BILLI GORDON'S

YOU'VE HAD WORSE THINGS · IN YOUR MOUTH · S

COOKBOOK

PUBLISHED BY WEST GRAPHICS

© 1985 by
West Graphics
R. West Productions, Inc.
576 Natoma Street
San Francisco, California 94103

Printed in the United States of America

ISBN 0-9614979-0-4

2 3 4 5 6 7 8 9 10 edition

EDITOR & ART DIRECTOR

R. West

TYPOGRAPHY & DESIGN

Augustus Ginnochio

PHOTOGRAPHY

Ken Towle (unless otherwise noted)

BILLI GORDON'S

YOU'VE HAD WORSE THINGS · IN YOUR MOUTH · S

COOKBOOK

TABLE OF CONTENTS

*My cooking is often referred to as yo-yo cooking because the recipes
found in this book will make your drawers drop down to your knees
and pop back up to your neck.*
—B.G.

INTRODUCTION

I'M THE AUTHOR, and I'm a NAP (Negro American Princess). A NAP is kinda like a JAP only instead of getting a nose job you get a clerical job.

Several things motivated me to write this cookbook, one of them being my great altruistic nature, another being my grave concern for the future of America. People are eating at so many fast food joints these days I wouldn't be surprised if the next generation of children was born on sesame seed buns with game tickets in their hands.

It is time to start switchin' in the kitchen again, and out of the goodness of my big, luscious heart, I have decided to share the recipes that have been handed down in my family (a family known for cookin') from generation to generation. A great many of these recipes come from the old country (Detroit).

I'm a very logical person, so I have taken a very logical approach to this book; I'm also a very truthful person, so I have taken a very honest approach. Now let's face the facts: when do you use a cookbook? Not every night, not even every other night—as a matter of fact, the only time you're ever concerned with a cookbook is when the meal is very important. Therefore, I have divided my recipes into four basic categories, categories which, I believe, cover the reasons (if the truth were told) we are compelled to use a cookbook. They are: **Seduction** dishes, **Motive** (I need this job/raise/part) dishes, **Destitution** dining and **Revenge** dishes.

Now, there are also a few other thangs, that I need to discuss. Case in point—*thang*. I must explain to you the difference between a thing and a *thang*, especially since I often refer to myself as a *big, luscious woman-thang*. It's not merely a matter of pronunciation. The difference is... well ... let me just give you some examples: homegrown is a thing, Hawaiian is a thang; a cup of coffee is a thing, a gram of Peruvian marching powder is a thang; Princess Diana is a thing, Diana Ross is a thang.

Julia Childs is a thing, I am a thang.

Furthermore, about the names of the vegetables. I really wanted to put the vegetables into two separate sections—whitefolks' vegetables and blackfolks' vegetables. But my agent reminded me that this is LA, in the 80's, and we're all liberal out here. There are Negroes, Negresses, Negrettes and Negrines (Old Negroes) living everywhere. And besides Mexicans do all the heavy labor these days.

Well, far be it from me, a liberal University of Michigan alumnus, to be conservative. So I decided to give all of the vegetable dishes women's names, like Suzie, Jane, Debbie, Patty, Amy, Kathleen, Kay, Jill, Muffy, Ann and Brooke. Also Ronita, Edwina, Mozella, Rocharda, Lonette, Theola and Glo.

Also, you'll notice when I refer to seduction dishes I refer to seducing him/her or both because, let's face it: it's a brand new day, and if you can't comprehend people seducing more than one person at a time, you obviously do not need to be reading this cookbook. 'Cause this cookbook is written for the girl (figuratively speaking, of course) who realizes a girl has got to do what a girl has got to do, and a woman must do the rest, honey.

Sinskey

"So, on the eighth day, God said, let my people greazze,
And as she crossed her big legs in the mornin' breeze,
She said let there be red beans, and let there be rice,
Let there be biscuits, don't make me say it twice."

SEDUCTION

SEDUCTION DISHES. Be careful with these thangs. These dishes are not to be made unless you mean serious business, 'cause honey, the seduction recipes will make a man tatoo *welcome* on his chest, crawl up to your bed, and say "I know I don't make enough money to deserve you but I can lick my weight in trading stamps!" Now you know I'm a luscious black, radical woman-thang, and I have used these dishes to seduce some white men (bless their Republican hearts) whose idea of liberal is dating a Canadian.

Case in point; Dempsey Webster Pemsford III—a man who thought NAACP stood for Negroes are Actually Colored Pollacks. Dempsey was so conservative he would get out of the shower to pee, but one bite of *Josette Florimbi Passion Pasta* and, sugar, this man was singing, "I wish they all could be colored girls." I had to get a peace bond out on that thin-lipped, Brooks Brothers boxer short wearing, balding, blonde fool to make him leave me alone.

Another example of the power of a seduction dish is the courtship and wedding of one of my girlfriends, Big Belinda Quinn. Now, I love Belinda dearly, but if Moses had seen her as a baby there would've been another commandment, 'cause Belinda looked like Cleveland in a pamper—and she grew up to be an even uglier woman. Child, her lips look like a life raft; if she stuck her head out the window of a speeding car, her lips would beat her to death, not to mention that the poor child's teeth point towards every major city in America. Honey, Big Belinda Quinn went on a cross-country trip. She stopped in Nebraska and went out into a cornfield to take a picture, and scared the crows so bad they brought back the corn they stole the year before. Anyway, Big Belinda Quinn snagged a man that is so hot, when you say his name your lips blister. I kid you not. This man is 195 pounds of dynamite with a long fuse. And this man married Belinda! Why? The Rip Tide Seafood Breeding Bisque. It brought him to his knees.

I'm telling you, I rest my case; if an ugly woman like Big Belinda Quinn can snag a man like that with this Breeding Bisque be careful honey, cause it's some powerful stuff. 'Cause Big Belinda Quinn did not look like a bride on her wedding day; she looked like a pidgeon that got caught in a badminton game. That fine man still said "I do" and the minister said "I'm sorry to hear that." Enough said, on with the recipes.

KILLA

I call this recipe "Killa", 'cause honey, it is deadly. This recipe will lay a prospective victim, oops, I mean romantic partner out, as soon as he/she or both walk through the door.

1 large artichoke
1 tbs vinegar (cider)
6 prawns
1 tbs olive oil
1/2 tsp salt
3 tbs vinegar (clear)
1 gallon water
1 quart water
2 tbs tarragon vinegar

2 tbs minced green onions
1/4 tsp minced tarragon
6 ounces chive flavored cream cheese
2/3 cup freshly grated Parmesan cheese
2 tbs cream
1 tbs diced shallots
2 tbs minced chives
1 dash cayenne pepper

First steam the prawns until done, and then put them in the fridge to chill. Then grab a small pan and slap in the tarragon vinegar and minced green onions and boil these suckers on high heat until the vinegar evaporates. Combine that mixture with the chive flavored cream cheese, minced chives, shallots, Parmesan cheese and dash of cayenne pepper, and I do mean dash. Stir in cream to thin it to a dipping consistency. Then throw her in the refrigerator and let her chill for at least 3 hours, but no more than five days.

Meanwhile, take the artichoke and cut about 1/2 inch off the top, and trim away all the pointy ends and tacky parts. Immerse her in one gallon of water and three tablespoons of vinegar to preserve her color. (Not everything's color is so steadfast.) It only takes a few seconds. Then bring 1 quart of water to a boil, throw in the remaining ingredients, and slap that artichoke in the pot, to boil for 45 minutes.

After the artichoke is done, arrange the leaves in concentric circles on a large platter. Place the dip in the center in a small dip dish. Then in a tall large stem glass, filled with crushed ice, arrange the shrimp by hanging them, tail outward over the sides. Serve the two together. It's the appetizer of death, honey.

TINGLES

Honey, this recipe will make Nancy Reagan go Greyhound. So you can imagine what it will do to a date.

3 ounces softened cream cheese
6 ounces smoked oysters
1 tbs dry Sherry
1 tbs fresh onion juice

1 tsp grated celery
1 tsp minced chives
1 tbs mayonnaise
1/2 tsp paprika
1 box Melba Toast rounds

Mix together all the ingredients, except the chives and Melba Toast. After the mixture is evenly blended, sprinkle the chives on top and chill.

Then, just before your righteous blond(e) arrives, spread the mixture on the Melba Toast rounds, sit on back, and think of love in terms of checkers . . . 'cause after serving this, if you're not careful, you'll get your Mason-Dixon line tore up, child.

LUSTETTES

When a girl looks out the window at her neighbor's panties hanging on the clothesline and realizes that life ain't fair, she has no choice but to turn to a recipe like this to even the score.

12 large mushrooms
6 tbs butter or margarine
   softened
1 clove garlic, pressed

1 cup crab meat, minced
4 tbs shredded jack cheese
2 tbs dry white wine
1/3 cup cracker crumbs

Take the stems off of the mushrooms (and don't throw them away—mushrooms are too expensive to be wasting). Melt butter and brush it over the caps of the mushrooms. Then stir the remaining ingredients together until well-blended. Place the 'shrooms in a large baking dish, with the cavity up. Place equal amounts of filling in each 'shroom and slap 'em in the broiler. Broil for about 400 seconds (3 minutes or so), serve these girls warm, and watch out!

CHERRY POPS

This dish is so easy to make you can do these tasty, colorful appetizers while you're fixing your colorful hair.

1 basket cherry tomatoes
1 can smoked oysters

1 tbs freshly grated
   Parmesan cheese

All you do is slice each tomato horizontally near the bottom, stuff in a smoked oyster, and sprinkle with a dash of Parmesan cheese.

Trust me, simple, yes, but Cherry Pops hit the spot . . . and I'm not talking about your stomach.

DARK DIVA

Like so many things of darkness and substance (e.g. moi) this little number will do a man in.

1/2 gallon chocolate ice cream
2 trays of ice cubes
1 fifth of 151 rum

cinnamon sticks
ground cinnamon

Take 8 scoops of chocolate ice cream and put it in the blender. Add four or five ice cubes, 1½ cups of 151 rum, and blend on a high speed until it's the consistency of a milk shake. Add 2 teaspoons of cinnamon. Blend again for one hot second, on high, until the cinnamon is mixed through.

This little cocktail tastes like it has virtually no alcohol in it, because of the strong influence of the chocolate and the cinnamon. It's perfect for those "summer love" seductions.

One blender-full should make four drinks. Put a cinnamon stick in each cocktail for a decoration, and serve in a large stem glass.

This is the perfect drink for the man who doesn't necessarily like alcohol, or for the man who thinks of himself as a little boy. Jocks love this drink. It's like a chocolate shake, honey.

HOTS

Let's just say the name of this dish speaks for itself.

1 tbs pimento
1 tbs chives, minced
1/2 cup freshly grated
   Parmesan cheese
4 minced green onions
5 tbs mayonnaise

1 tbs Gouda cheese, grated
1 tbs Muenster cheese
2 tbs diced shallots
1 dz cocktail size pieces of
   French bread

Mix everything together except the French bread. While you're mixing, toast one side of the French bread. When it's done spread the mixture on the untoasted side of the bread, and bake in the oven at moderate heat until lightly browned. Serve hot.

TEMPTATION

Imagine it honey...''Temptation'', your best dress and that lonesome cowboy up the street whose been dying to hit your dusty trail.

4 egg yolks
1 cup milk
3 cups (about 12 oz.) finely
   shredded Fontina cheese

1/2 ounce white truffles
1 tbs chives
1/2 cup Monterey Jack cheese
1 loaf of French bread, cubed

Simmer the egg yolks in the top of a double boiler with the milk. When the mixture thickens enough to coat a metal spoon with a thick velvety layer, stir in everything but the bread cubes.

When all but a few pieces of the cheese are melted, remove from the flame and leave sitting over hot water for ten minutes.

The cubes of crusty bread are sensuously dipped into the sauce with the fingers.

FIRE

Use this on that silver haired daddy whose let the snow on the roof put the fire out in the furnace.

bourbon

151 rum

This one may sound horrible, but you just have to trust me. This is the cutest little trick, and it will just make your evening something very special. But be forewarned, this is not a beginning-of-the-night drink! This is a darkness drink. This drink must be served in a dimly-lit room.

Pour two shots of bourbon in a glass, then pour one shot of 151 on top. Light the 151 on fire. I love a flambe, don't you? Then you hand it to him and let it go out. (Be careful not to let it burn too long or the glass will crack.)

After the flame is out, add ice... and let another fire begin.

NEGRITA

This cocktail will make a man praise boogie, and I don't mean disco, sugar.

Fresh squeezed orange juice
Fresh squeezed pineapple juice

100 proof vodka
ice cubes

Take some ice cubes, slap them in a blender; pour in about a cup of orange juice, a cup of pineapple juice, and a cup of vodka. Put the blender on liquify and blend until the ice cubes are crushed. Then throw this little number in a large glass (a hollowed pineapple is even cuter than a glass), garnish with an orange slice and a pineapple chunk, and call it a day.

TUSHETTE

When you need a full on tush and all you got is a tushette,
try this instead of pads, honey.

orange juice
apricot nectar

rum
vodka

Take the fresh squeezed orange juice about 1½ cups, add 3/4 cups of apricot nectar, 2 shots of rum, and 2 shots of vodka. You'll have a delightful little cocktail that will sneak up on you, while you sneak up on somebody else . . .

RHUMBA

This will make 'em want to go south of the border, honey.

tequilla
vodka
orange juice (fresh squeezed)

grapefruit juice (fresh squeezed)
lime

Take 1/2 cup of grapefruit juice, add 1/2 cup of orange juice with a shot of tequilla and a shot of vodka, pour over ice and squeeze a lime wedge on top for a garnish.

LURE

Honey, this recipe will get you and your man closer
than two ticks on a chihauhau's tail.

12 ounces condensed green
   pea soup
12 ounces half and half
3 tbs very dry sherry

6 ounces crab meat
22 ounces condensed tomato soup
1 dash cayenne pepper
1 tsp grated celery

Combine all the ingredients, except the crab meat and the sherry. Cook for four minutes over medium heat, flake in the crab meat, add the sherry, and cook for another minute. Proceed with caution, girl.

PASSION POTAGE

Honey, this recipe will make a rattlesnake try to breed with a buggy whip.

1 tbs butter or margarine
2 cups canned pumpkin
2½ cups orange juice
1/4 tsp salt
1/2 tsp powdered ginger

1 tsp grated orange peel
1/4 tsp pumpkin pie spice
1 cup light cream
2 tbs minced onion
1/4 tsp allspice

Start this little doozie by melting the butter in a saucepan. Add the onions, and cook those girls until they're tender. Add the remaining ingredients, except the cream, and simmer about ten minutes—being careful to mix all the ingredients well. Then stir the cream in slowly, being certain not to let the soup come to a boil. And, child, step back.

CONQUISTADORESS

Honey, this is a "Nuptials On My Mind" recipe.

22 ounces of condensed
    tomato soup
11 ounces condensed consomme
1 cup sour cream
1 tsp grated shallots

1 tsp grated celery
1/2 cup sherry
2 tbs chopped parsley
4 tbs each of sour cream, chives
    and paprika

Start out by stirring the tomato soup and the consomme together with 1 cup of the sour cream, and the sherry in a tasteful saucepan. Make sure you get those girls smooth. Then add the shallots, the celery, and the parsley. Heat until they simmer. Then top each individual bowl with a teaspoon-full of sour cream, some chives and paprika for a garnish. It will lay a man out, sister.

DIRTY DEED

Serve this girl, wear a festive dress, and your worries are over, and his have just begun 'cause after you've served this, girl. . .think mink.

1 pound lean ground beef
1/2 cup quick cooking oats,
    uncooked
1/2 cup grated onions
1/4 cup wheat germ flakes
2 eggs
1 tsp salt
2 tbs vegetable oil

2 tbs flour
1 cup half and half
2 tbs drained capers
2 tbs grated bell pepper

Combine the wheat germ, beef, onion, egg, salt, pepper, Worcestershire sauce, 3/4 cup of milk, oats, bell pepper, and shape into 36 meatballs. Brown the meatballs in hot oil. Stir the flour into the drippings. Add remaining milk and half and half. Add salt to taste to gravy. Also add capers, and speaking of capers, start planning yours, honey. Cook slowly, stirring constantly, until thickened. Put meatballs in gravy and simmer.

ECSTASY

Honey, this recipe will work a man like a constipated Nazi foreman.

1½ pounds sirloin tip, cubed
3/4 cup finely chopped shallots
3/4 cup cracker meal
   (no offense to honkettes,
   honkines, and honkesses)
1/8 tsp garlic powder
1¾ tsp salt, divided
1/4 tsp pepper
2 tbs chives
2 tbs celery
1½ cups milk
3 tbs butter or margarine

1/4 cup flour
1 cup sour cream
10 ounces condensed consomme
3 tbs tomato paste
1 tsp Worcestershire sauce
1/2 cup cooked rice
1 cup pitted black ripe olives,
   cut in wedges
2 cups hot cooked noodles
3/4 cup mushrooms

Combine beef, onion, cracker meal, celery, chives, garlic powder, 1½ tsp of salt and pepper and milk. Shape into 10 or 12 cakes. Brown slowly in butter. Combine the flour and sour cream; add undiluted consomme, tomato paste, Worcestershire sauce, and remaining salt. Pour this over the meat cakes. Cook slowly for ten minutes. Add the sherry and ripe olives. Mix it gently. Serve it with the rice, noodles, attitude and a cheap perfume.

RAPTURE

This dish will make a man walk through a forest fire, on a wooden leg, carrying a backpack full of motor oil to get to you.

1 large rabbit cleaned and cut up
1 cup cooking oil
1 cup flour

1 large onion diced
1 cup diced mushrooms
salt and pepper

Salt and pepper the rabbit pieces. Then bread them with the flour. Heat the oil in a large skillet, throw the rabbit in and brown it, honey. Then take it out after it's done. Put two tablespoons of the flour, the onion and mushrooms in the remaining oil; brown. Add two cups of water, then put the rabbit back in and simmer for twenty minutes on low, while you simmer for twenty minutes on high.

SNUGGLE

This recipe will snatch a faggot away from a Judy Garland movie, so you know it's got to be good.

2 large red squirrels, cut up
   and cleaned
1 cup flour
1 cup cooking oil

1 cup diced onions
2 cups mashed potatoes
1 cup diced mushrooms

Fry the squirrel in the oil after coating it with flour. Take it out of the skillet after it is done. Pick all the meat off of the bones, put two tablespoons of flour in the oil, and add the mushrooms and onions; brown, put the squirrel back in, add two cups of water, simmer for 20 minutes on low, salt and pepper to taste, then pour over the mashed potatoes. . .vondah-bah dah'ling!

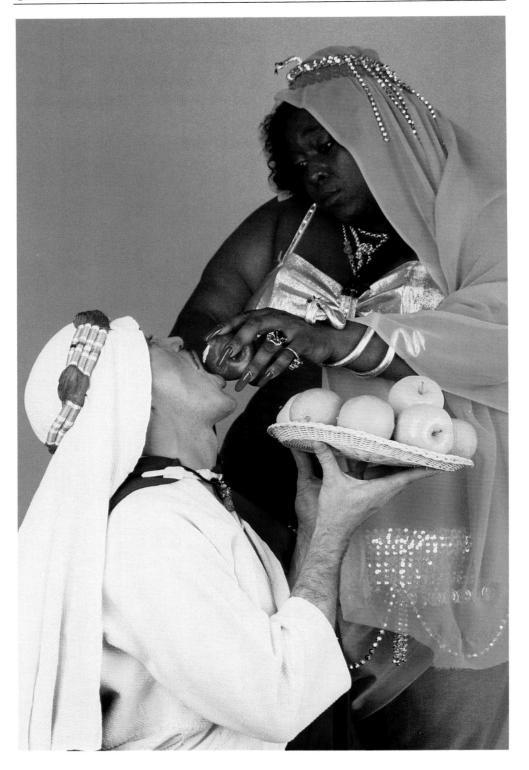

"An apple I give thee, Rubys, furs, and gems for me."

RIPTIDE SEAFOOD BREEDING BISQUE

This, honey, is the fish soup of death. This stuff is so good it ought to be illegal.

1½ pounds swordfish
1/2 pound shark
1 pound medium sized raw shrimp
16 ounces clam juice
3 tbs olive oil
2 medium onions finely chopped
2 medium carrots, thinly sliced
1 pound scallops
1 large green pepper, seeded
   and chopped
2 cloves garlic
1/2 tsp crushed red pepper

1/2 tsp dry basil
1/2 tsp thyme
1/2 tsp whole coriander seed
   crushed
8 whole clams in the shell
1 lemon, thinly sliced
14 ounces of chicken broth
3/4 cup white wine
2 bay leaves (take out immediately
   after cooking)
11 ounces, tomato puree

Before I start, let me just say this; after cooking the bay leaf, take her out and throw her away! Never serve food with a bay leaf in it! I lost my last husband, Bruce, that way. He swallowed a bayleaf whole, it cut his throat like it was a pigfoot...and, honey, all that man left me was alone. The only thing I got at the reading of his will was gas.

In a large pot, heat the oil over medium heat and saute the onion, garlic and green pepper until the onion is soft. Stir in the tomato puree, clam juice, wine, broth, bay leaves, red pepper, basil, thyme, coriander, lemon slices, and carrots. Simmer uncovered for 10 minutes or so. Add the clams. Cover and simmer until the clams begin to open then add the shrimp and fish to the broth. Cover and simmer until the shrimp turns pink and the clams open fully.

Amen.

CARESS

*Slap this little number on the table, and watch your date fall on his (her) knees.
I assume you can take it from there.*

2 pounds skinless flounder or
  sole fillets
2 tbs lemon juice
1/2 cup madeira
2 tbs butter
2 tbs all purpose flour
1/2 tsp Dijon mustard

1/2 tsp chicken stock base
1/3 cup whipping cream
3/4 cup shredded Swiss cheese
20 ounces chopped spinach
  (cooked)
2 tsp chives
1 tbs dry sherry

Preheat your oven to 400 degrees. Fold the fish fillets in half and arrange side by side in a large shallow baking pan. Mix the madeira, sherry and lemon juice and pour it over the fish. Cook for approximately 10 minutes. Then drain off the liquid into a measuring cup, and add enough water to make a total of one cup. Cover the fish, and set both it and the liquid aside.

Melt the butter in a pan, stir in the flour and the chicken stock base, and whip—gradually adding the poaching liquid, the chives and the whipped cream. Cook it until it thickens, stirring periodically. Add half of the Swiss cheese.

Arrange the spinach in a casserole dish, slap the fish on top of the spinach, pop your dress tail, cover with sauce and the remaining Swiss cheese, and bake for 7 minutes. Then cross your legs and wait (but not too long).

COOCHIE

*This girl will pucker a man's lips up so tight with pleasure, he'll have to use a
shoe horn to take an aspirin.*

1 pork roast
1 can cream of mushroom soup
1 can celery soup
1 can cream of onion soup
4 cups stuffing mix
1 medium chopped onion

3 tbs chopped celery
2 eggs
1 soup can of hot water
salt and pepper
6 large mushrooms

Mix all of the ingredients together (except the pork roast) until well-blended. Then enshrine the pork roast in the dressing, and bake until the roast is done (approximately one hour) and look out! Lust, wanton passion, and ecstasy are on the way!

BLISS

*She's simple, but she'll put a killing on a man.
A typical Italian girl, honey.*

1 package fettucini
16 ounces sour cream

2 jars black caviar

First, boil the fettucini until it's done. Then drain it, let it cool, and combine with the sour cream and the caviar. Then set back and wait for your Italian Stallion to start hoofing it.

HEFFA

*This is so good your guest will get to smackin' their lips so much
the people next door will get up to dance.*

1 tbs butter
1 duck (about 5 pounds)
1 cup muscatel
2 tbs red currant jelly
1 cup chicken broth
1/2 cup seedless green grapes

1 tsp ginger
1/2 tsp cinnamon
3 tbs shallots
1 tbs grated celery
1 tbs grated carrot
1/4 cup brown gravy
    seasoning sauce

First, brush the duck with the seasoning sauce. Then slap her in the refrigerator for 2 hours. Saute the onions, carrots and celery in butter. Add the other ingredients, including the duck and excluding the grapes. Cover, and simmer on the stove for an hour. Remove the duck, and boil the sauce on high heat until it thickens down to about 3/4 cup. Strain the sauce over the duck and add the grapes. Honey, believe me, this little number will hurt a man.

BUNCOMBE

*This will make those Italian boys think about
their mamma, and you know how those boys like their mammas.*

1 frying chicken, cut up
1/2 cup flour
1/3 cup vegetable oil
1 clove garlic
1 bay leaf
2 onions, diced

1 can tomatoes (16 ounces)
6 ounces tomato paste
1/2 pound sliced mushrooms
1 tsp salt
1 dash cayenne pepper
3/4 tsp oregano

Coat the chicken with flour. Brown it on all sides in the oil. Add all the remaining ingredients except the oregano. Simmer for 30 minutes. Add the oregano and simmer for another twenty minutes. A dish for all those Italian Stallions, this little number will make them think about their mamma.

SINTHIA

*I call this dish Sinthia, because there's a heifer in my life named Cynthia, who's
from southern descent, and whose stolen many husbands from me with this
very dish. . .well, not actually stole, but. . .let's just say Cynthia and I are wives-
in-law. . .anyway—*

1 cup flour
1 frying chicken, cut up
1 cup diced mushrooms

2 cups milk
2 onions, diced
1 cup cooking oil
salt and pepper

Salt and pepper the chicken. Then flour it. Heat the oil in a frying pan and add the chicken. Fry until it's golden brown. After removing the chicken, save about 3½ tablespoons of the oil in the pan. Put two tablespoons of flour in the oil, and all the onions. Brown the flour until it's about my color. Then add the milk, turning the heat up high, to make a heavenly gravy. Add salt and pepper, the chicken, and the mushrooms, and simmer on a *very low* heat for half an hour. Honey, this dish will bring a strong man trembling to his knees, crying, and saying, "darling please." Use liberally on construction workers, grips, gaffers, truckers, and cops.

DELIVERANCE

Save this recipe for the man who fades back with the football of your heart, and throws a long pass over the goal posts of your love. (Touchdown?)

2 pheasants, (preferably wild)
2 cups flour
1 tbs brandy
1 cup diced mushrooms
2 tbs flour
1 cup diced onions
3 tbs chopped celery

1 can cream of mushroom soup, condensed
1 cup oil
salt and pepper
2 cups water
1 box stuffing mix
2 eggs
1 cup cooked brown rice

First take the oil and heat it in a skillet. Cut one pheasant into pieces; flour the pieces after you salt and pepper them. Fry until they're golden brown.

In a large bowl, in the meantime, combine the stuffing mix, the brown rice, some salt and pepper, the eggs, the chopped celery, the cream of mushroom soup, and half of the cup of diced onions.

When the pheasant is done, debone it completely. Take one third of the meat and put it in the bowl with the stuffing, and mix thoroughly.

Now pour all but 3½ tablespoons of the oil out of the frying pan. Add two tablespoons of flour, the remainder of the cooked pheasant, the mushrooms, the remainder of onions, salt and pepper. Cook the ingredients until the flour is nice and brown. Then add the brandy and the water. This will make a wonderful sauce. The sauce of death, honey. Let this simmer on the lowest heat possible for 35 minutes, constantly stirring so it doesn't stick. Be careful not to let too much of the water evaporate. You want a good gravy consistency. 35 minutes may be too long, depending on the type of stove you have and how much control you can get out of it.

Anyway, you stuff the other pheasant with the stuffing. Take the remaining stuffing and put it around the pheasant in the roasting pan. Mop the pheasant with butter and bake her for half an hour on 375 degrees.

After that heifer is done, put her on a platter, pour the sauce over the girl, add the surrounding stuffing and ohladeedah!

PAVI ELLE

This could make Princess Diana summer in El Salvador.

5 eggs, separated
1/2 pound swiss cheese
1 tsp chives, diced
1 tbs diced shallots
1/3 cup evaporated milk

1/2 tsp salt
4 tbs flour
1/2 cup finely diced mushrooms
1/4 pound Gouda cheese
1 tbs Dijon mustard

Pour the evaporated milk into the top of a double boiler. Then add the flour, salt, mustard, and beat until smooth. Place over the boiling water. Beat until slightly thickened (about 5 minutes). Grate the cheese into the mixture and stir occasionaly with a rotary beater until the cheese has melted and the mixture has gotten thicker, honey. In fact, beat it until it's smooth. Remove it from the heat, add the egg yolks one at a time, beating after each yolk. (Now wash the beater thoroughly. . . even if you're a slob you must wash the beater thoroughly or the egg whites, which you're about to beat, won't stiffen.) Add the chives, shallots and mushrooms to the cheese mixture, then beat the egg whites in an ungreased dish until they're very stiff. Fold in the cheese mixture, bake in a preheated oven at 300 degrees for one hour, and be prepared to serve this girl immediately!

JOSETTE FLORIMBI PASSION PASTA

This dish could make Idi Amin sing the Yale Alma Mater in Gaelic.

1 package fettucini
2 cups eighthed tomatoes
1 pound medium deveined shrimp
  (cooked)
2 tbs olive oil
1 dash oregano
1 pound scallops, cooked
  and chilled

1 cup button mushrooms, cooked
1 jar red caviar
1 jar black caviar
1/2 cup diced green onions
1 cup wine vinegar
1 dash rosemary
1 dash basil
1 dash thyme

Cook the fettucini, and let it cool. Mix the oil and vinegar and spices together, along with the red caviar. Then you take the remaining ingredients and mix them with the fettucini. Pour the wine vinegar dressing over it, mix thoroughly, let it chill for two hours, and, what will happen in five minutes will last for a lifetime (better make that ten minutes).

SUPPLING

Honey this recipe will make Barry Goldwater get kinky with Coretta Scott King.

22 ounces condensed cream of
  asparagus soup
6 tender young asparagus spears
22 ounces cream

1/2 cup cheese croutons
2 tbs diced pimentos
1 dash cayenne pepper

Combine all the condensed soup and the cream in a pot, and mix while cooking over low heat. Chop the asparagus spears into small pieces and add them, cooking until they're tender. Add the diced pimentos just before you finish cooking the soup. Add the cayenne, also.

Chill the soup for at least four hours, then garnish with the cheese croutons and have mercy!

HEDONNA

Child, marriages have been made on less stuff than what's in this recipe.

3 cups water
1/2 tsp Worcestershire sauce
1/2 cup nonfat dry milk
8 ounces lobster meat
1 tbs lemon juice

1 tbs lime juice
2 tbs chives
3 tbs flour
1 tbs salt
1/8 tsp black pepper

Pour the water and the Worcestershire sauce into the top of a double boiler. Sprinkle nonfat milk, flour, salt, pepper over the top of the water. Beat those suckers until they're evenly blended. Cook over boiling water, constantly stirring her until she starts to thicken (kinda like an old ingenue). Stir in the onions and the lobster meat. Then, right before serving, add the lemon and the lime juices in that order. Honey. . .marriages have been made on less.

THE BOSKOE CLOSE

You can substitute the cherries with any fruit . . . well not any, I mean pineapple or blueberries but not your hairdresser.

2½ cups all purpose flour
1 tsp salt
1 cup shortening
6 tbs water

1/2 pound butter
1 cup sugar
2 tbs flour
1 pound pitted sour cherries

Okay, combine the butter, the two tablespoons of flour, the cherries and the sugar. Cook them on low heat in a sauce pan until they're thick.

Then take the 2½ cups of flour and sift into a bowl. Resift the flour with the salt. Take this mixture and cut the shortening into it with a pastry knife (or two butter knives held in the same hand) until the mixture is about pea-sized in grain. Then you add the water slowly until everything sticks together. Now, here comes the trick . . .

The trick in pie crusts is to only have to roll it once, and handle it as little as possible. Take the dough, divide it in half; carefully roll each piece out until it's large enough to cover the pie plate.

Pour in the cherry mixture; cover the cherry mixture with the top crust. Press the crusts together by pushing down along the seam with a fork. (If you're anal, now's a good time to work off some neuroses. Try to keep the lines all the same length and perfectly even all around the pie.)

In the center of the pie, punch your date's initials (if you know his/her/their last name/names) using little toothpick holes. This is an especially effective practice when seducing men, because my theory (tried, tested and proven) is that if you kiss a man on the ego first, he'll let you kiss him anywhere else after that.

THOU SHALT NOT

This dish will make a rabbi move to Cairo.

1 box frozen spinach
4 eggs
1 cup diced onion

6 slices bacon
1/2 cup diced mushrooms
salt and pepper

First fry the bacon until it's very crispy. Then take it out and break it into tiny bits. Save the bacon grease. Put the spinach, onions, mushrooms, salt and pepper into the grease and fry until the onions are soft. Then put the bacon and eggs in, turn off the skillet, and stir constantly until the eggs are well-mixed with the spinach and thoroughly cooked. And thou shalt reconsider.

MOJO

This mojo will work when yours won't.

10 pound pail of chitterlings (chitlins)   1 pound of hog mawls

First you have to clean the chitlins. You do that by scraping the soft fatty material on the inside of the chitlin. Do this very well. Rinse them thoroughly, throw them in a pot that has about 5 quarts of boiling water and cook them on low, for 2 hours. Add the hog mawls after the first hour of cooking. Honey! It be good.

SULTRINA

Girls, this recipe is like a man with no arms or legs . . . trustworthy.

3 eggs lightly beaten
3/4 cup dark corn syrup
3/4 cup sugar
1/4 cup molasses

2½ tsp vanilla
1 cup pecan halves
1 pie crust
3 tbs melted butter

Make a pie crust. (Use the recipe from the Boskoe Close, only cut the measurements in half 'cause you only need a single crust.) Put the crust in a pie pan. Spread the pecan halves along the bottom of the pan. Combine the eggs, corn syrup and molasses; mix well. Add sugar, mix it well. Add the vanilla, stir it well. Let everything stand for five minutes.

Melt the butter, and stir it into the syrup mixture. Pour this mixture over the pecans. Wait for the pecans to rise to the top. Bake at 375 degrees for 45 minutes and, honey, stand back! What is about to come out of your oven is lethal! It's so good, I'm surprised it's not contraband.

SUCKLING

This dish could make Joan Collins wear stretch pants.

1 cantaloupe, diced into bite size
 pieces
1 quart strawberries, fresh
3 peaches diced into bite sized
 pieces

1 honeydew diced into bite sized
 pieces
1 quart chocolate milk
1 pound of your favorite chocolate

Melt the chocolate into the chocolate milk, and cook on a low heat until it makes a wonderfully thick, rich, and sinful chocolate sauce. Then arrange the fruit in a ring on a large serving dish.

Put the sauce in the "bowl" in the middle of the ring of fruit, serve. Dip the fruit with your fingers into the sauce and eat, or feed it to each other. Picture that, honey . . .

"Oooo, he said she was easier to make than instant coffee."

MOTIVE

MOTIVE DISHES, or I need this job/raise/part dishes, are for those meals when you have a definite purpose. A purpose much more serious than seduction. Motive dishes are for those cozy little meals when your boss, or some prospective director/producer, etc., has got you sitting at the table lying to him— talking about how good he looks in his new toupee, 'cause you know the rent is due and he must pay it. Not to mention that the gas man showed up pounding at your door earlier that same day, with a wrench in his hand, talkin' about turning off your gas, and you got a pound of bacon in the refrigerator that you know you cannot fry in a crockpot.

Motive dishes are subtle but to the point. For example, my friend, no-neck Andrea Goldberg, started as a file clerk at Megla Insurance. (Well, actually, before she got the job at Megla she was in retail... We won't really go into that. Let's just say she had kissed so many sailors her lips used to go in and out with the tide.) Anyhow, she invited her boss over and served him the Chi Chi Lopez en croute, and today Andrea is sitting up in the executive suite, doing absolutely nothing but signing letters and watching one soap opera after another in a Halston mumu with brie on her breath. And Andrea is no mental giant. As a matter of fact, you tell her to make up her mind and she powders her forehead. A motive dish was all the genius she needed, honey. Need I say more?

Well, as a matter of fact, I might as well say more—this is off the immediate subject, but I think it's very relative to the overall issue of cuisinal excellency. And, besides, this is my book and I can say whatever I please...

You know, one of the most fascinating things about food is how creative we have been in how we've learned to eat it over the years. Now, who would've thought that when the first woman stalked the woods, 4,000 years ago, and came upon an egg, she'd gnaw a hole in the shell, suck the yolk out, and that this moment was the cerebral grandparent to the souffle?

Not only that, I've often marveled at how it was that certain, obscure food sources came to be food sources in the first place. For example, watercress. I would just love to meet the heifer that found that girl after walking for miles along some creek, nibbling at each of the hundreds of different plants that populate a creek bed. Imagine picking up all the different mosses and grasses and shrubs and taking a bite until you got to watercress and saying, "That's it! That's just what my salad needs."

Or honey. Honey is bee dukey (feces). Now, dukey is dukey. There is certain nutritional value in dukies, I suppose. But how is it that the person who discovered honey figured out that bee dukey was sweet, and a good food source, as opposed to, say, cockroach dukey... or pig dukey. Certainly pig dukey is alot more abundant, and if you're gonna eat dukey, what difference does it make whose dukey it is?

Which makes me think of milk. (Milk and honey—you have to understand how my mind works.) Has it occurred to you just *what* was the man who discovered milk, doing down underneath that cow? Think about it. If you had never heard of milk, or tasted it, would *you* get down underneath a cow and just start pulling on things? Thank God it was a cow and not a bull. If it had been a bull, imagine what we'd be putting on our cereal in the morning! Not to mention the price of butter would be sky high, and cheese would just be out of the question.

And what do you think the cow must have felt like? I mean, how would you feel if a cow came up to you and started pulling on things and drinking what came out? And the bees ... can you imagine what the talk must have been like around the hive when they looked out and saw the most intelligent animal on the planet (alledgedly) in the latrine lapping?

Honey... a motive dish is more essential to a girl's well-being that she may imagine. Considering where we came from, where we're going, where we're at and what we must do.

NEW JERUSALEM PATÉ

This appetizer is big in Prime time t.v. circles.

6 ounces deviled ham
1 cup chopped ripe olives

1 tbs grated cooked onions
6 ounces liver spread
1 tbs fresh squeezed lemon juice

Combine the deviled ham with a cup of the chopped olives and 1 teaspoon of the grated cooked onion. Combine the liver spread with the lemon juice and the remaining onions and olives. Place each mixture in an identical but separate mold. Then stack the two on top of each other after several hours of serious chilling.

An appetizer like this will not only prove you're abounding with creativity, but it will also appeal to the person's roots. . . regardless of what they are.

GIMMES

This dish will take a man's fancy like Grant took Richmond.

1 envelope unflavored gelatin
3/4 cup clam juice
1 cup Rhine wine
1/2 tsp cayenne pepper
1/4 tsp Worcestershire sauce

1/2 tsp salt
12 small scallops
12 small shrimp
  (chilled and cooked)
12 Melba Toast rounds
mayonnaise

First take half of the clam juice and soften the gelatin in it. Then heat the other half of the clam juice, and add it to the gelatin until the gelatin dissolves. (Gelatin is like a young blonde, such a pain, but so showy in the end.) Cool the mixture, add the Worcestershire, salt, cayenne, and wine.

Place one shrimp and one scallop in each cup of a miniature muffin tin. (If you don't have a miniature muffin tin, you must have some gay friends—so borrow one—a muffin tin that is. If you don't have any gay friends, people aren't being honest with you, and you better dash out to the department store and buy your own muffin tin, 'cause it's going to be a long, lonely life.)

Add just enough gelatin mixture to barely cover the seafood. Chill until firm. Unmold. Spread mayonnaise on the Melba Toast rounds and top with the gelatin cups.

COWEENA McDERMIT

If that new leotard won't get you your raise,
this is what you need.

6 ounces cream cheese
4 tbs chives

1 tbs shallots
1/2 cup toasted pine nuts

This is a very simple appetizer that is extremely tasty and can be used when you want to impress upon your guest how hard you've been working. You can go on about how simple this appetizer is for hours, all the time interjecting what elaborate things you would've done if you'd had the time or money. (Know what I mean?)

Mix the cream cheese, chives and shallots together. Mold into any form you might like. Then cover the outside with the toasted pine nuts, and garnish with crackers and radishes, and then see if this *raises* your standard of living.

BEVERLY HILLS MOUSSE

I picked this little gem up from my friend Bon Bon when I was on sabbatical in Milwaukee at Hebrew A&M (Accounting and Medicine).

8 ounces chicken livers
8 ounces calves liver
8 ounces beef liver

6 hardboiled eggs
3 large yellow onions
1 average container of schmaltz

The Beverly Hills Mousse is a must if you plan on getting anywhere in this world. First take the schmaltz, which is chicken fat, and melt it in a frying pan.

Then cook the onion, which you have sliced into large pieces, and cook until soft. Don't brown them! Cook the livers, but make sure that they're not quite done.

Take a food grinder (and I don't mean food processor but an old fashioned food grinder) and grind the onions, then the livers, and the eggs. Add a dash of salt and pepper, and a bit of the schmaltz, to achieve a smooth consistency and, honey, call it a day. Mold it, chill it and throw it on a plate. Garnish it with crackers.

NEGRETTES

This recipe is for the girl whose trying to feather her nest with a little "cash down".

6 ounces of shredded
   cheddar cheese
15 medium pitted green
   stuffed olives
1/4 cup of all purpose flour

1 dash cayenne pepper
2 tbs butter or margarine, softened
1 tbs minced anchovy

Beat the cheese and butter until they're well blended, like a good southern whiskey. Then stir in the flour and cayenne. Wrap a teaspoon-full of dough around each olive, covering completely, being careful to sprinkle just a tad of anchovy on the inside of the dough before you wrap.

Bake these girls in the oven for 5 minutes at 400 degrees. Serve hot, and honey, you've made points.

MACHIAVELLIANETTES

While your guest is carrying on about how tasty this little delicacy is, you hit the sucker with the fact you need a raise because an impoverished homosexual broke into your apartment, redecorated, and stole your blow dryer.

6 ounces smoked salmon
5 ounces cream cheese
1 tbs finely diced shallots
1 clove pressed garlic

1 chopped green onion
1 dash cayenne pepper
1 dash salt
1 dash black pepper
12 Melba Toast rounds

Mix all of the above ingredients together, except the Melba Toast rounds. Chill for an hour, then spread on the toast rounds. And speaking of spreading . . . . . .

COCARICOCOARICO

Great for those of you who live in the snowbelt to serve in the wintertime, and the fall, and the early spring, and whenever else it's cold out there.

2½ quarts milk
2 cups Nestle's Quick

1½ tsp cinnamon

Another drink for the underaged. Take the mild and the cinnamon and the Quick and mix them all together until blended thoroughly. Heat the mixture and serve hot, (or the drink can also be served hot).

MOSCOCIOUS

The quickest route to a nice juicy part is through a producer's drunken stupor. Try this one on for size.

12 ounces apricot nectar
2/3 cup sugar
2 tsp whole cloves

2 cinnamon sticks
1 large bottle Chablis
1 cup Muscatel

Combine the nectar, sugar, spices. . . then simmer for about 15 minutes. Strain that sucker. Add the wines. Heat but don't boil. Serve this hot, and it will loosen up the evening.

OLD TANNENBAUM

This will go just perfectly while you're saying, "Deck the halls with Credit Suisse Bars. . . falalalalalalala"

4 eggs, separated
1 cup sugar
2 quarts milk

1 bottle cream sherry
2 cups rum
nutmeg

Beat egg yolks until they're thick and lemon colored. Then beat in 3/4 cup of sugar, slowly. Continue until the sugar is dissolved. Add the milk, sherry and rum. Chill this mixture. Then beat the egg whites like they're step-children, and fold in the sugar. Fill a punchbowl and sprinkle the top with nutmeg.

TINSEL TOWN BLUES BISQUE

Serve, and pretend it took all day to make.

1 tsp curry powder
1 large can evaporated milk
11 ounces cream of mushroom soup

6 large chopped mushrooms
1 tbs chopped shallots
1 tbs chopped chives

Curry is like a hot man. It has to be handled very carefully or it's just terrible. First blend the curry with a little of the evaporated milk until it makes a smooth paste. Add the remaining milk slowly; combine the mushroom soup, the shallots, the chives and the mushrooms, being careful not to bring the mixture to a boil.

SYCOPHANTIQUES

This is a great intro into telling your boss you fell asleep smoking at your desk and burned up the bookkeeping records for the last quarter.

1 pound lean ground lamb
1 tsp cumin
1 tsp chopped fresh mint
1/4 cup finely minced green onions

1/4 tsp pepper
1/4 cup fine dry bread crumbs
2 eggs
1 tsp grated lemon

Mix the above ingredients together, then form into little meatballs. Cook in the oven at 400 degrees for 15 minutes. Save the juices to serve the meatballs in. Wonderful for working greedy men.

MONKIES AND BABIES

I call this monkies and babies because monkies and babies are the only things I find cute, and every Honkess, Waspess, Negress, and Jewess thinks their 10-year-old monsters are cute. And this is a drink for those Honkettes, Waspettes, Negrettes, and Jewettes, who are pulling whips out of your dresser while you're asking their daddy for a raise.

6 ounces frozen orange juice
1½ cups Nestle's Quick
1 quart chocolate ice cream

1 quart chilled club soda
1 fresh orange

Mix the orange juice concentrate and the Nestle's Quick. Stir it until it gets smooth. Put it in 8 soda glasses. Add a scoop of ice cream to each glass. Add the club soda and give it to your boss' kids.

REBECCA

This is a meal for an old-fashioned man with a brow full of sweat, a bunch of roses in his hand, and a trunk full of credit cards.

1 pound pork chops
1 cup flour
2 tbs flour
6 large mushrooms
1 cup cooking oil
salt

pepper
1 medium onion
7 medium sized potatoes
1 tbs milk
1 tbs butter

First peel and boil the potatoes. While they are cooking, put the flour in a paper bag and salt and pepper the chops to your taste. Then shake 'em up in the bag, adding more flour, if necessary, to coat them. Fry in the oil. After the chops are brown, take them out of the oil and set them aside. Now put the onion in the oil (after you've chopped it) with the mushrooms (diced), two tablespoons of flour, 1 teaspoon of salt and 1/2 teaspoon of pepper. Cook this mixture until the flour is browned. Then add two cups of water. This will make a wonderful gravy, if you stir it. Put the chops back in the gravy and simmer for 20 minutes on low.

Now stop cooking the potatoes, remove them from the water, add the butter and the milk, and whip them until they're extremely smooth.

Serve the chops and the gravy over the potatoes, and good gocious!

PHOEBE

Aw shucks is all you need to say when you slap this girl on the table.

12 ounces croaker fish (whole)   1 tbs chili powder
2/3 cup finely chopped pecans   2 eggs
2/3 cup dry bread crumbs   3 tbs butter

Heat your oven to 500 degrees. And while the oven is heating, combine the chili powder, the pecans, the bread crumbs, and chives. Beat the eggs like they're step-children. Roll the fish in the egg, then in the crumb coating. Meanwhile, melt the butter in a baking dish large enough to accommodate the fish. After you've coated a fish, throw it in the dish, coating each side with the butter and cook for ten minutes or until golden brown.

"I've been eatin' so much fish, I'm breathin' through my cheeks."

FAITH

A boss has got to have faith! So if your boss needs a little faith, and your name ain't Faith, then slap this on the table... honey.

12 ounces condensed green
  pea soup
1 tbs grated onion

1/2 cup white wine
1 cup milk
4 slices crispy crumbled bacon

Combine all the ingredients except the bacon, and cook them on a low heat until they're well-blended. Do not allow the soup to boil. Garnish each bowl with the crumbled bacon bits, and call it a day, honey.

ELLEN BETH

When you serve this, be prepared to throw your head back and act real white.

6 tbs butter
3 tbs diced shallots
1 cup sliced almonds
1 cup coarsely crushed unseasoned croutons

1/8 tsp pepper
4 large mushrooms
2 tbs breadcrumbs
4 fillets lingcod

First preheat the oven to 375 degrees. Then grab a skillet and saute the shallots, almonds and mushrooms. Remove from the heat and add the croutons and the pepper. Mix well.

Put 2 fillets in a greased pan. Spread the stuffing evenly over the top of them. Then put the other two fillets on top. Then you bake those girls for 35 minutes uncovered and jump back, sugar.

BILLI

Obviously with a name like this recipe has, it is a heavy, rare, succulent, dark treat, that is certain to bring a man trembling to his knees and leave him eternally grateful and forever satisfied.

1 bottle smokey flavored
  barbecue sauce
1/2 cup molasses
1 lemon squeezed
1/2 cup vinegar
1 clove
1 tsp lime juice
1 tbs soy sauce

2 whole spare ribs
1 bottle instant smoke flavor
1 bottle teriyaki marinade
1 quart water
1/2 cup vinegar
1 quart of water with 2 tsp salt
  added and 1 tbs vinegar

Obviously, since I put my name on this recipe, I believe in it. It is the best.

Combine the first 7 ingredients, cook over a low flame for 5 minutes.

Then take the spare ribs, and put 1 bottle of instant smoke with 1 bottle of teriyaki marinade and 1 quart of water, and let them marinade in a cooking dish. Add the 1/2 cup of vinegar and let it all sit for 24 hours. Then take the water, salt, and vinegar mixture and put it in a bottle. Cook the ribs on charcoal briquettes for two hours, very slowly, constantly basting with the bottled mixture. During the last 45 minutes of cooking, apply the sauce to the ribs, turning frequently, and, honey, there it is; the best dish known to womankind.

"One good man, it ain't much Lord,
but it's every little thing."

MISS JONES

*This girl is simple, but think back to high school: didn't the simple girls
always seem to have a date?*

1 pound boneless catfish fillets	salt
3 cups white cornmeal	1 cup cooking oil

Salt the catfish to your taste. Put the cornmeal in a brown paper bag, put the catfish in too, and shake it all up while you're heating the oil in a black iron skillet. Throw that catfish in the skillet when the grease gets hot! Cook her on medium heat, covered, until she's brown on each side... turning maybe twice.

Child, a man will wear some catfish like this out. See, sometimes, you can impress them with mousses, etc. But a good man needs to know that a woman's cookin' goes on down past the oven to the flo'.

KIT

*This dish is good on politicians, as it is best used in laying the seedy,
the shady, the needy and the greedy to rest.*

4 whole chicken breasts
1/4 cup butter
6 ounces thinly sliced truffles
2 cans condensed cream of
    chicken soup

1 minced garlic clove
2 tbs chives
1/8 tsp crushed rosemary
2/3 cup half and half

Take two large skillets and divide the ingredients equally between them. Brown the chicken
in butter; remove. Brown the mushrooms. Stir in the soup, garlic and other seasonings. Add
the chicken and simmer for 45 minutes, stirring occasionally. Slap this girl on the table and
good gocious Amanda Amin!

LUCINDA

*Honey, all you need is this dish, a pair of pumps and a little poppin'
of that dress tail and the case is closed.*

1 frying chicken, cut up
4 tbs butter
16 pearl onions
salt
pepper

3/4 cup beer
1/4 cup tomato sauce
1/4 cup cream
1/4 cup mushrooms

First brown the chicken in butter, adding the onions and the mushrooms. Add the remaining
ingredients except the cream. . . bring to a boil. Cover and simmer for 1/2 hour. Then let this
chill, and skim off the fat after it has risen to the top. Then stir in the cream, reheat, and you're
in business, child.

REGINA

*Lamb is to rich white men, what buying wholesale is to Jews. So honey if you
plan on making points. . . lay a little lamb on 'em.*

1 crown roast of lamb (16 chops)
1 garlic clove, crushed
1 tbs chives
1 tsp mint jelly
1 tbs vegetable oil

1/2 tsp salt
1/2 tsp pepper
1 tbs crushed onion
hot mashed potatoes

Rub the lamb crown with the garlic. Sprinkle it with the salt and pepper. Make a mixture out
of the vegetable oil, mint jelly, chives and crushed onions. Rub it on the crown. Then roast at
425 degrees for 30 minutes. Fill the center with hot mashed potatoes. Honey, this too will lay
a date out to rest.

CHI-CHI LOPEZ EN CROUTE

Not only will this heifer do the job, but she'll do it cheap,
that's why I named her Chi Chi.

1 can chili beans
1 can kidney beans
1 can pinto beans
1 pound chopped beef
1/2 pound chopped pork

1 can tomato sauce
2 onions
1 clove garlic
1 tsp cayenne pepper
4 tbs chili powder
3 cups cracker crumbs

Combine all the ingredients except the cracker crumbs in a large baking dish. Spread the cracker crumbs on top and bake uncovered for 45 minutes. Good when you don't have a lot of money—but do have a lot of ambition.

"There's one more than one way to hold office."

ANASTASIA

Good gogliocious! That's exactly what your date will say when you lay this impressive number on the table, sit back, cross your legs and strike a pose...

3/4 pound skinless perch fillets
3/4 pound crab meat
2 egg yolks
2 eggs, separated
3/4 cup half and half
3 tbs all purpose flour
1/8 tsp freshly ground nutmeg
1 tbs lime juice

1 tbs brandy
1 cup whipping cream
1½ cup clam juice
1/2 cup dry white wine
2 tbs lemon juice
1/2 cup half and half
2 tsp cornstarch
1 tbs dry sherry
1/2 pound small cooked shrimp

Needless to say, this girl does not come easy. It's one of those two part numbers. What you do is combine the clam juice, 1/2 cup of white wine, the lemon juice in a sauce pan and boil her, uncovered until it's reduced to about 1 cup liquid.

Then beat 2 egg yolks like you're a mad leather queen, until they're light yellow; blend in the cornstarch and 1/2 cup of half and half. Using a wire whip (sounds kinky doesn't it?), gradually blend the hot mixture with the egg mixture. Return the whole thing to the sauce pan and cook her over low heat, stirring the girl constantly until she thickens. This should take between five and ten minutes. Then slap the tablespoon of sherry and those shrimp in there, honey, and lawd hammercy! And this is only the sauce, child! Set it aside.

By now you have preheated the oven to 350 degrees. In a blender combine the fish and crab. Blend until it's a paste. Put it in a bowl. Add the 4 egg yolks, one at a time, stirring the mixture until smooth after each one (obnoxious, but necessary). Beat in the half and half, flour, nutmeg, lime juice and brandy. (And have a shot of brandy for yourself—you deserve it!) Whip the cream until it's stiff, and fold gently into the fish mixture. Beat the egg whites until those girls are stiff, and fold them into the fish mixture. (Have another shot of brandy... don't worry, your date will understand.)

Butter six two-cup capacity ramekins. Distribute the fish mixture evenly among them. Place the ramekins in shallow baking pans; fill the pans halfway with hot water. Bake uncovered for twenty-five minutes. (And while you're waiting, you might as well kill that bottle of brandy.) Just before the Moussettes are done, heat the sauce gently, never allowing it to boil. Let the Moussettes cool ten minutes before serving them with the shrimp sauce. When you slap this dish on the table, make sure you have the bridal shop on the phone... 'cause, honey, honey hush!

PEARLIE MAE WONG

This girl will slant anyone's eyes.

1 tbs butter
2 cups precooked rice
1 cup strained cooked green peas

2 tbs diced pimentos
1/2 cup sauteed onions

Cook the rice according to the directions on the package, then melt the butter in a frying pan. Combine the remaining ingredients with the rice, and cook in the butter for 5 minutes, stirring frequently. Rots of Ruck, honey.

QUICHE LAWANDA

They say that real men don't eat quiche. . .but honey please.
Real men eat anything, and that's why they're real men.

6 eggs	3 tbs chives
1/2 cup cream	2 tbs diced shallots
2 tbs flour	1/2 tsp salt
1 cup grated swiss cheese	1/2 cup diced mushrooms
1 cup grated Gouda cheese	1 ready bake pie crust

I'm sorry honey, but I just don't believe in making pie crust for quiche. For my blueberry pie, maybe, but for quiche never.

So take the eggs and cream and the flour, and blend them very well. Then pour them into the pie shell.

Mix the remaining ingredients together and add them to the shell.

Slap that girl in the oven, and bake on a moderate temperature (like 375 degrees) for a half an hour, or until the quiche is done.

Throw this quiche on the table, and see if your man eats it.

ANITA BAXTER

This dish is so white it has to be cooked wearing a simple strand of
pearls. . .nothing more, nothing less.

1/4 cup butter	1/2 tsp salt
1 cup diced celery	3/4 cup water
3 tbs chopped onion	3/4 cup orange juice
8 ounces precooked rice	2 tsp grated orange peel
1/2 tsp sugar	1/2 tsp anise
	1/4 cup diced pineapple

Melt the butter in a sauce pan, add the celery and the onion. Cook it until it's tender. Add the remaining ingredients except the orange peel. After cooking, let the rice stand 10 minutes. Sprinkle with orange peel and praise boogie, honey!

ROXANNE McKINLEY

For the Puerto Rican version of this dish, cook this dish in pointed-toed shoes.

6 tbs butter	1 tsp Worcestershire sauce
6 tbs flour	1 tbs diced chives
1/2 tsp salt	3 cups milk
1 tsp chili powder	9 hardboiled eggs, quartered
1/2 tsp cayenne pepper	1/2 cup diced onions

Melt the butter, blend in the flour, salt, chili powder, cayenne pepper, Worcestershire sauce, onions and the chives (in that order). Add the cold milk all at once. Cook this over low heat until it gets thick, and then add the eggs. This should be the second hottest thing he/she puts in his/her mouth that night.

HUSHED INFERNO

This is for that full figured girl who knows she's gotta land that weightlifter if she plans on getting carried over the threshold.

1 cup light cream
1½ cups chicken broth
2 tbs lime juice

1 ripe avocado
1 dash cayenne pepper
1/2 fresh lemon, squeezed

First, peel the avocado and take out the pit. I usually plant the pits; they're easy to grow and great plants.) Place the pulp in a blender and add the chicken broth and the lime juice. Put that sucker on puree! Add the rest of the ingredients, and blend it very well. Chill for at least 4 hours. It makes a great cold soup.

Try this one on your favorite muscleman and watch the pecs react.

Sinskey

"We're talkin' cream of hunk, honey"

MUFFY

For a ghetto version of this trés suburban dish, substitute sweet potatoes for the yams and don't blot off the excess oil.

6 medium yams cooked and peeled
1 egg beaten (preferably by a
servant)
1 tbs whipping cream

flaked coconut
vegetable oil for frying
1/2 tsp ginger
1/4 tsp nutmeg

Mash and peel the yams while hot. Add the nutmeg and ginger. Combine the egg and cream. Shape the yams into tiny tasteful balls, roll in the coconut, and fry in deep vegetable oil until brown. Blot excess oil on a paper towel, (nothing about Muffy should ever be greasy).

*"Now hear this Miss Jill, Muffy and Ann
What you be doin' any girl can."*

ALICE BROWN

Honey when there's a man or money in question—go ask Alice.

2 cups chopped spinach
1 cup onions
1 pound shaved ham
4 deviled eggs

1 cup grated Swiss cheese
2 cups milk
2 tbs butter
2 tbs flour

First, make a cheese sauce by melting the butter with the flour and a little of the milk (enough to make a mushy paste), then add the rest of the milk. Cook on low heat until it thickens, add the cheese. Put the spinach and onion in a greased shallow baking dish. Top with the shaved ham and deviled eggs, pour the cheese sauce over the whole thing, and bake at 350 degrees for one side of your favorite Diana Ross album.

SUZIE

This valley dish is totally Bitchin'!

1 pound drained canned beets,
diced
1/4 tsp salt
3 tbs prepared horseradish

1/2 cup dairy sour cream
3 cups coleslaw
2 tbs chives

Combine the above ingredients, except the coleslaw, and mix together well. Chill for an hour. Mold the coleslaw into a ring and slap those beets in the middle.

JANE

Like a true Jane this dish is kinda homey and plain, but it gets by.

1 can condensed cream of
  celery soup
3/4 cup cream
6 ounces truffles

3 cups cooked brussels sprouts
2 tbs chopped onions

In a double boiler, combine the soup and cream, add the rest of the ingredients and cook until the onions are as tender as the night . . .

AMY

As suggested by the name this dish's simplicity is second only to it's caucasianicity.

1 pound can green beans
2 tbs butter
1/4 tsp rosemary

1/2 tsp basil
1/4 tsp dill
salt
pepper

Drain the liquid from the canned beans into a sauce pan, and boil until it's reduced to half the amount. Add the beans and cook until they're warm. Melt the spices into the butter and pour over the beans. Salt and pepper, throw your head back and act real white.

BROOKE

Eat this dish, while wearing topsiders once a week and you'll be blond in no time.

2 cups grated zucchini
1 tbs parmesan cheese, grated

1 tbs butter

Cook the zucchini in a sauce pan until tender. Melt the butter, blend in the parmesan, and pour over the zucchini, and blame it on the democrats.

KAY

For the black version of this dish substitute muscatel for the sherry.

2 cans petit pois (tiny peas)
1 pound can small white onions

2 tbs sherry
1 can cream of celery soup

Pour the peas and the onions in a pan, along with the juices from the can—add the other ingredients—and cook slowly. This dish is real simple, but then so is Kay.

PATTY

The only thing more Patty than this dish is navy blue coullottes.

2 heads cauliflower
2 hard-cooked eggs
2 tbs minced parsley

1 tsp basil
1/2 cup bread crumbs
1/2 cup melted butter

Separate the cauliflower into caulettes, add boiling salted water, and cover. Cook until tender, drain. Chop eggs, sprinkle over the cauliflower with parsley. Toast the bread crumbs in the butter, add the basil, and spread over the top and then throw this sucker in the trash, 'cause if you can get a raise with cauliflower, then you need a new job.

DEBBIE

For an authentic Mexican twist, prepare this dish in a hubcap.

2 packages frozen brussels sprouts,
    cooked
1/2 cup butter

2 tsp Dijon mustard
1 tsp Worcestershire sauce
1/2 tsp thyme

Melt the butter; blend in all the other ingredients except the brussels sprouts. Steam them, then pour the butter sauce over them, and then contemplate breeding Mexicans with octopuses so they can pick more brussel sprouts.

JILL

To quote your average Jill, "Golly, wow! Jeepers it's good!"

4 tbs butter
2 pounds canned whole
   honky white potatoes

1 dash cayenne pepper
paprika

Melt the butter in the skillet. Drain the potatoes and put them in and saute. Sprinkle lightly with cayenne and generously with paprika, then call Merrill Lynch.

BRENDA BEA

This dish, with a face long enough to run the Kentucky Derby on, will put your raise in the bag.

butter
8 eggs, separated
8 slices cooked ham
8 slices french bread

Dijon mustard
3/4 pound swiss cheese
1 small onion, finely diced
1 tbs chives

Butter the bread on one side, and toast it in a skillet. On the untoasted side, spread the mustard, top with a slice of ham and a slice of swiss cheese. Beat the egg whites until they're stiff. Make a hollow in the center of the egg whites. Place some of the diced onion in the hole, then top with an egg yolk and sprinkle the white with the chives. Place on a cookie sheet and bake at 350 degrees until the whites are lightly browned, and then start counting the green.

KITTY KEVORKIAN

Serve this delicacy, named for the queen mother, in pink pudding dishes wearing nothing less than cocktail sequins.

2 packages vanilla pudding
1/4 tsp nutmeg
1/4 tsp cinnamon

1 tsp 151 rum
3 bananas

Combine the spices with the dry pudding mix. Then make the pudding according to directions. Throw in the rum and the bananas (after slicing the bananas thinly). Let sit in a refrigerator overnight.

Serve it with a lot of attitude.

There once was a buxom beauty
Who danced on the beach with her cutie

WANDA TITLEBAUM

Miss Titlebaum will hold office, Bernice.

2 cups uncooked macaroni
1/4 pound butter
6 ounces swiss cheese, grated
6 ounces jack cheese, grated

6 ounces cheddar cheese, grated
6 ounces Muenster cheese, slices
salt
pepper

Cook the macaroni (in salted water if you like). Strain the noodles and put them in a large baking dish, add the butter, and stir in all the cheeses except the Muenster. After all the cheeses have melted, lay the Muenster slices on top and brown in the oven for a couple of minutes and the rest can be added to your resume.

KATHLEEN (KATH)

Like your basic Kath, this dish doesn't have much to it but for some strange reason rich white men like it.

2 pounds canned green beans
2 tbs finely chopped onions
1 can cream of mushroom soup

1/2 cup toasted slivered almonds
1 dash cayenne pepper

Drain the liquid into a saucepan and add the onion. Boil the liquid rapidly until there is only 1/2 cup left. Gradually stir in the soup, add the beans and almonds. A favorite of young ambitious republicans.

ANN

For more original "Ann type" flavor, make this dish in a tennis outfit.

3 tbs wine vinegar
1/2 tsp pepper
1 tsp grated lemon peel

1/4 tsp celery salt
1 tbs grated onion
sliced tomatoes

Combine the ingredients and let stand overnight. Like Ann, this is a locker-room favorite.

BORITA PEREZ

For a more authentic Mexican taste—steal the ingredients for this dish.

1 cup regular uncooked rice
1 clove garlic, minced
1 medium onion, chopped
1/4 cup vegetable oil

1 pound stew beef
1 tbs chili powder
1 pound canned tomatoes
1 green pepper diced

Cook the rice in a frying pan in the oil until it's golden brown, add the onion, garlic, green pepper and beef. Cook until the beef is browned. Then stir in the rest of the ingredients. Add salt and pepper to taste, then turn your eyes toward Ensenada.

MACHO PUFFS

When all else fails, slip 'em some drugs. Immoral? Yes. Illegal? Definitely. But honey it's as practical as hell.

2 cups flour
1/2 cup shortening
1 cup cooking marijuana
1 cup sugar

1 cup melted cooking chocolate
1/4 cup cocoa
1 tsp cinnamon
1 tsp baking soda
1 tsp water

Cream the shortening and the sugar; add egg; beat them like they're red-headed step-children. Sift the marijuana, flour, cocoa and cinnamon three times. Add the melted cooking chocolate to the shortening mixture, then add the flour mixture. Dissolve the baking soda in the water and add this too. Put the batter in muffin tins. Bake at 375 degrees in a preheated oven for 15 minutes.

Sinskey

He will eat this.

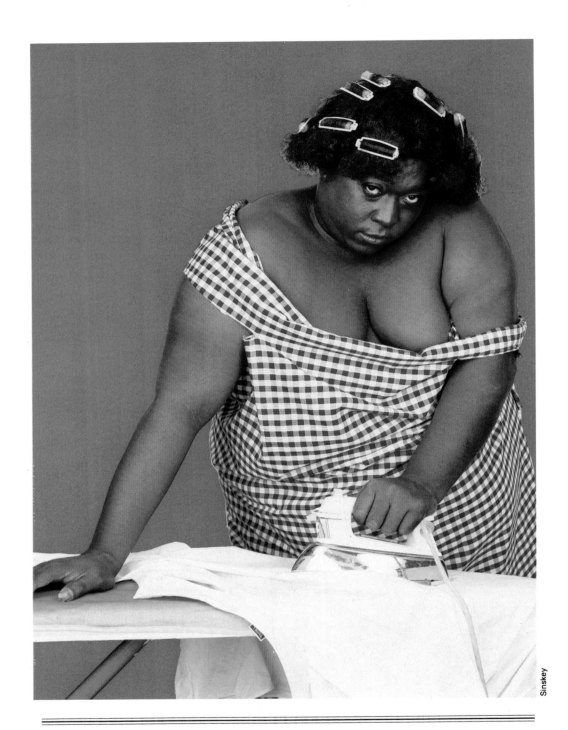

Sinskey

Yah, well you know southern California
Must look like hope to my dog and my ma
But this here can of plain wrap lasagna
Look like the one in L'il Rock, Arkansas

DESTITUTION

YOU may think that I'm a suave, sophisticated, polished, urbane Hollywood glamour-puss. To a certain extent, you're right. Granted, the city lights and city nights have eroded away a certain amount of my earthy maidenhood... Let it not be said, however, that I can't relate to the impoverished masses, because I am a part of it. Was it not I who said, "Let them eat Plain Wrap?"

Anyway, the bottom line is, times are hard. If you're like me, you have more bills than a flock of geese. And we're not alone. Old people have been eating so much cat food that Friskies is getting ready to put George Burns on the can. *Times are hard.* People are looking for eggs in cuckoo clocks.

Which explains why there are no "Sweet Thangs" in the Destitution Dining Section, just as there are no casseroles in the Seduction section. My point being that if you can seduce a man with a casserole, you don't want him, and if you're destitute you certainly don't need to eat dessert. Face it sweetheart, the rent will soon be due, and you know you might have to jump out on the streets and go into retail to pay it. Therefore, you must watch your figure. I suggest if you want dessert, have some fruit. And I don't mean the boys at the hair salon either... Although that is an idea...

The key to destitution is being proud. There are a lot of things worse than being destitute, like being pregnant by Idi Amin and the obstetrician predicts quintuplets; or like finding yourself in the middle of Beirut wearing nothing but a Yamaka.

And speaking of yamakas, honey do I have a destitution tale to tell you, that will explain to you in philosophical essence why a woman must have, among her repertoire of skills, tricks, trinkets, potions and charms, the knowledge of destitution dining.

It all happened on a dreary night, a few years ago when I was but a mere lass of, well it's not important how many years, but a lass, nonetheless. I was dating a big Italian number, by the name of Hank De Stallionini. I'm sure you've heard of the Stallionini brothers. Anyway, honey that Hank used to eat like his gums were leaving town in the morning and taking his tongue with them. At the time my bank account was so low that the bank was charging me interest. So I didn't know what to do when I received the call that my beloved was done mixing concrete and was on his way over to pay a call on his lovely and hopefully someday soon, bride to be (moi).

Well I went to the store with the last of my pentois, yes I had scraped my hope chest cleaner than an anal retentive nun. Well there was just nothing in my price range. Although I must confess my budget was tighter than a middle class Jew in a recession.

I don't know how it happened but somehow, and not of my own doing mind you, a 10 pound bag of potatoes and a sack of onions found their way into my brassiere, and the strangest thing, a 15 pound ham, somehow managed to get lodged between my legs underneath my dress. Well you can imagine the shock, horror and dismay, not to mention chagrin that overwhelmed me when the store manager pointed the unusual goings on out to me, four blocks down the street, after a minor altercation that hospitalized no more than four carry-out boys and two checkers.

Well for some reason they felt the need to involve the authorities, which happened to be readily available because we just happened to be in front of a donut shop. I swear, girls, if it wasn't for bad luck, sometimes I think I wouldn't have no luck at all. Know what I mean?

Child, they took me down to the Police Station, and they handcuffed me to this sway-backed, drop chinned, tight eyed, low neck, loose nostrilled, back alley concubine, by the name of Seville, who said, "Hi, my name's Seville," to which I sarcastically replied, "lovely name." She told me that her "business manager" named her after his favorite car. A real gem huh? Well do you know that this heifer had the unmitigated gall to make some comments about the fact that I was a full figured woman-thang, and that anybody that had the audacity or the thigh grip to walk out of a grocery store with a 15 pound ham in between their legs, plus run four blocks from the store manager without getting caught, hospitalize four carry-out boys and never drop the ham deserved to go to jail. I told her that at least I didn't get arrested for having one foot on one corner, and one foot on the other corner sucking up men in the middle of the block. She said a girl had to make a buck. I said, "I guess you weren't making enough money with those roller skates on, that mattress on your back, giving curb service and green stamps. She said, "Listen Ponderosa, if you ever fell down you'd rock yourself to sleep trying to get back up." I told that droopy jawed, mega foreheaded, nuclear lipped hussy that her coiffure looked like the southwest corner of a mandril's behind after the monsoon season, halfway through a drought. She told me that the only way I could ever see my toes was via satellite. She also said that I oughta rent myself out to large cities and let them wrap me in gauze and run through a few tunnels once a month to clean them out. I responded by giving her some heavy PAD (Poise, Attitude and Disapproval). She said "well honey, sell some shade space at parades, anything but you just got to stop stealing hams."

I told that heifer that her tits point towards hell. You know she had the uncurtailed nerve to say, so does your navel. Well they booked me, and Hank De Stallionini got me out on bail. Now see if I had known how to cook the Destitution dishes I would have never had to have gone through the awful experience of meeting that dreadful Seville!

On that note... I give you Destitution Dining, Dah'ling... proud dishes to help you hold your head up high while your fortunes are slowly and steadily sinking. Honey ...

LA GUIENA POQUITO SON RUBIA

Even though you may not be able to afford to change your mind...this little dish will make your guests think you have Gucci bones.

6 large eggs (hard boiled)
1/4 tsp salt
2 tbs mayonnaise

1 tsp mustard
1 tsp ketchup
1 dash pepper

This is always a very welcome, yet cheap appetizer.

Cut the eggs in half, lengthwise; pop out the yolks. Mash them and combine with the remaining ingredients. Then refill the white halves with the mixture, and sprinkle the tops with paprika for decorative reasons. If you're really poor, lay the eggs yourself.

CASTRO BEV

The Castro Bev is a delightfully cheap and cheerful little fruit number, hence its name.

1 apple
1 pear

1 banana
2 oranges

The trick to the Castro Bev is in the presentation. You must cut the apple in thin, thin slices, then do the same with the pear and the oranges as well.

Arrange them on the plate in the most beautiful array possible, with the banana sliced lengthwise and the slices cut into fours. This is for the year the IRS sends you a sympathy card.

POMPETTES

Eating is like sex. It's all in the mind, basically. It's not what you have to serve it's how you serve it...sugar"

1 cup unpopped popcorn
1/4 cup melted margarine or butter
1 clove pressed garlic

2 tbs grated Parmesan cheese
1/2 tsp onion salt
1/2 tsp celery salt
1 dash cayenne pepper

This will really make them feel your poverty and marvel at your creativity. Especially when you've thrown in a few "it's all I really could afford's."

Anyway, all you do is pop the popcorn, pour on the butter, and mix with the four other ingredients and serve. A fool could do it... and has.

"It's a little known fact that most great cooks partake of a cocktail while they work!"

HOO DOO

The question is not "Hoo Doo," but who don't . . .

1 package great northern beans
1 ham hock
1 onion

1 tbs sugar
1 clove garlic
1 small piece salt pork (3 ounces)

The trick to destitution is planning it out. This bean soup seems expensive at first glance—the ingredients coming to well under $5.00, but still . . . anyway, it too, will last for days and days.

Combine the above ingredients in a large pot of water, and cook on medium heat for 3 hours. The only sad "T"about this dish is you can't cook with the gas you'll get.

MAME'S McKENZIE SPECIAL

In order to get the best flavor out of this recipe,
play scrabble while you're cooking it.

1 box macaroni & cheese dinner
1 can tuna fish
1/2 cup chopped celery
1/2 cup chopped onion

salt
pepper
milk
butter or margarine

Make the macaroni and cheese dinner according to instructions. Then, put it in a casserole dish, flake in the tuna fish, and add the onions and celery. Mix well, bake for 25 minutes at 375 degrees. And to quote Mame "If you don't like this dish you obviously don't have a sense of humor, and you're going to end up living in a trailer in down river Detroit with a shork neck husband named Otis."

SHIRLEY ANN

It's cheap and easy to make, but it gets the job done . . .
so typical of a girl named Shirley.

6 hardboiled eggs
2 tbs mayonnaise

1 tbs ketchup

Dice the eggs. Mix the remaining ingredients and you're in business, sugar, whether you need to be in business or not.

FUFU

When you've eaten so much tuna you go to breathin' through your cheeks,
try this recipe for a change up.

6 hardboiled eggs
1 tbs mustard
2 tbs mayonnaise

1 dash pepper
1 tbs grated onion
1 tbs grated celery

Grind the eggs in a food grinder, mix in the remaining ingredients, and the dish you have will be just too "Fufu."

MADGE JOHNSON

This recipe is for white women only.

8 ounces precooked rice
1 cup peeled, diced orange
2 tbs sugar

1/4 cup slivered almonds
1/4 tsp vanilla extract
1 dash cinnamon

Cook the rice and fold in the remaining ingredients. Wear a matching pastel jogging outfit while cooking this.

FRANNY DE MILLE

It's cheap, but cheap things can be good. I'm speaking from experience, honey.

1 package spinach noodles
parmesan cheese

Cook the noodles according to the directions on the package, then sprinkle with parmesan cheese. Slap some oil on your fingers and sit back and get greazzy.

EDWEENA

Hammercy, ouee, shucks!

3 pounds fresh collard greens
1 pound of kale
1 large onion
4 smoked ham hocks

1/2 pound fat back (salt pork)
3 parts fresh okra
1 banana pepper

First you bring to a boil a large pot of about 2 to 4 quarts of water. Throw in the hocks and the fat back. Then let that cook for about 45 minutes to an hour, covered. While she's cooking, wash and pick the greens, dice up the onions, the okra and the pepper; when the 45 minutes are up, throw the greens and the other ingredients into the pot, let it cook until the greens are dark, and the onion is tender. Just remember this, a catfish needs water and a girl needs greens.

ROCHARDA

When they talk about "meat and potatoes," honey, this is what they mean.

2 cups diced potatoes
1 cup diced onion
1/2 cup diced celery
1/2 cup diced zucchini

1 cup bacon fat
salt
pepper

Heat that (the bacon) fat in a skillet. Put the rest of the ingredients in the skillet; fry until the potatoes are very brown. This is proof of the old saying "the best things in life are almost free."

TUTHILL TONIC

Honey this will make a man sing 'Hang on Sloopy' if anything will.

1 package kool-aid
  (unsweetened)
1 lemon

1 cup sugar
1 tray ice cubes

Take the ice and kool-aid and put them into the blender. Peel the lemon and add it whole. Turn the blender on high and beat until the ice cubes have been crushed to death. Pour into a two-quart pitcher, and fill to the top with water. Very cool, honey, extremely trendy, mega-chic.

AGRIPOLA QUE MOHA

When you're as broke as the 10 Commandments, slap this on the table.

1 dozen celery sticks
1 dozen carrot sticks
2 large ripe avocados
3 tbs lime juice
1/2 tsp salt

4 canned green chiles
1 tbs grated onion
1 tbs pimento, chopped
1 tbs pomegranate seeds
1 clove minced garlic

Take the avocados, pit them, and scrape the insides into a bowl. Add the lime juice, salt, green chiles, grated onions, pimento and minced garlic. Blend until it's as smooth as a Harlem pimp. Speaking of Harlem pimps. . . . Then garnish with celery and carrot sticks, and sprinkle the top of the dip with pomegranate seeds.

CREAM OF GRIEF

Now this soup may not sound that cheap, but since you can eat this for a week, it works out to less than one cent per serving. That's cheaper than a female hooker in San Francisco.

4 cups milk
4 tbs flour
4 tbs margarine
2 tsp salt

1/4 tsp pepper
2 large onions
4 cups any
  (any vegetable you might have)

First in the soup pot mix the flour with some of the milk to make a paste . . . gradually add the rest of the milk and margarine, heating slowly on a medium heat. Add the onions, the pepper, the salt and any vegetables you might have. Cook on very low heat until the vegetables have all cooked to pieces. (Vegetables to consider are corn, carrots, celery, and basically anything that is in season and on sale except something rude like jicama or beets.)

LEE ANNE

*Like many a girl of southern descent this dish and her reputation
have been passed on from man to man.*

1 stewing chicken
2 cups flour
salt

pepper
1/4 pound margarine

In a large pot, start boiling the stewing chicken. In a bowl, mix the flour with the salt and
pepper, then add enough water until it gets to the consistency of gooey. Put the margarine in
the pot with the chicken. Then drop the flour mixture into the boiling water, in teaspoon-
sized bits. Let it cook until the hen is done, and prepare to shake a cuisinal tit.

DINA OSBORN

It's a cheap little number but it'll hit the spot, like cheap little numbers often do.

1 cup turkey meat, cooked
2 tbs chopped celery
2 tbs chopped onions
2 cups cooked rice

salt
pepper
1 tbs cooking oil
2 eggs

Heat the cooking oil in a pan. Combine the remaining ingredients together, put them into the
pan, and cook until the onion and celery are tender, while thanking God your name is not Dina
Osborn.

OSCEOLA JACKSON

Honey these grits will lay a rice dish to rest.

1 cup uncooked grits
1 cup diced shallots

1 pound swiss cheese
1/2 pound margarine

Saute the shallots in the margarine. Cook the grits according to box directions. Then, after the
grits are done, stir in the Swiss cheese (which you should grate) add the shallots and the
margarine. You know how rice will slant your eyes, honey, this girl will flatten your nose.

LONNETTE

The only greens better than these are the greens on money.

1 pound mustard greens, fresh
1/2 pound turnip greens
1/2 pound swiss chard

5 large turnip bottoms, quartered
1 pound fat back
1 pound pork neck bones

Boil the neckbones and the fatback in two quarts of water for a half an hour. Then throw in
the greens and go on about your business, 'cause honey, those greens will do the job, without
taking too many of your ducets, honey.

MOZELLA

It will be worth going out in the woods to pick Polk Salad, sugar Pie, honey bunch, sister Plum!

3 pounds fresh polk salad (a spinach
   type vegetable that grows
   wild in the woods)
1 onion diced

1 tbs baking soda
1/2 cup bacon fat
3 eggs

Into a pot of boiling water dissolve the baking soda, then throw the Polk salad in there and leave for 3½ minutes. Take it out, and, in a fresh pot of boiling water, boil it until it's limp and looks like cooked spinach. Heat the bacon fat in a skillet, add the onions, the Polk salad, and the eggs, and shimmy like your big sister Kate, and if you ain't got a big sister Kate, shimmy anyhow, honey.

*"Honey, I done eat so many greens . . .
When I went for a pregnancy test the rabbit bit me."*

TAMMY

Just like any Tammy that you've ever known, this dish is a little greasy, but it's cheap, so it has its place, honey.

1 can mackerel
1 onion
1 egg
2 tbs flour
2 tbs chopped celery
1 tsp black pepper
1/2 cup cooking oil

With the exception of the cooking oil, combine the above ingredients together. Shape into patties and fry in the oil. For a true Tammy effect cook this while wearing terri cloth hot pants.

TRUDY LE BEAU

Slap this heifer on the table and honey, money or not, you'll get by.

1 pound turbot
1 cup rice

1 can cream of mushroom soup
1 package small cooked shrimp

Cook the turbot ten minutes, on high heat, in a sauce pan with water. Boil the rice, and add salt if you like. Add the can of cream of mushroom soup to the drained and cooked rice. Break up the turbot and mix it in, and layer the top with the small cooked shrimp. Let chill for two hours in a refrigerator, and eat cold.

The turbot will take on the taste of the shrimp! And it will be like you've made a very expensive shrimp dish when, in actuality, you've spent no more than $1.00 for shrimp. This is a great pot luck dish, and honey a poor girl has to work those pot-lucks.

ANGIE LYNN

This is a dish for the girl who married the man who didn't have much upstairs but whose basement was packed.

4 eggs beaten
1 tbs shallots, diced
3/4 cup quick cooking oatmeal
1/2 cup chopped onions
1/4 cup chopped green pepper

1/2 cup milk
1 tbs soy sauce
salt and pepper
vegetable oil
1/2 pound ground beef

Combine the first 8 ingredients with the 1/2 pound of ground beef. Form into 8 flat patties. Fry the patties in the hot vegetable oil over low heat until brown on both sides, serve with rice, and call it a day honey, 'cause the tupperware party is over, Mary Beth.

DOCTOR ORANGE

This is just one of the things I'll teach you that your mamma didn't know about.

1 fresh orange
1 can orange juice concentrate

Take any frozen orange juice, follow the instructions on the can, put it in a blender, add one fresh orange to it and it tastes like fresh squeezed. Now, doesn't that alone make buying this book worthwhile, that and all the luscious pictures of moi.

LATANYA

Honey, hush. Honey, just hush!

1 cup white corn meal
3 large green tomatoes
salt

pepper
bacon fat

Cut the tomatoes into 1/8 inch thick slices. Then salt and pepper them. Bread them in the corn meal and slap them into a skillet that has about 1/2 cup of hot bacon fat. While you're cooking this, sing that old spiritual "Swing Low, Sweet Bacon Fat."

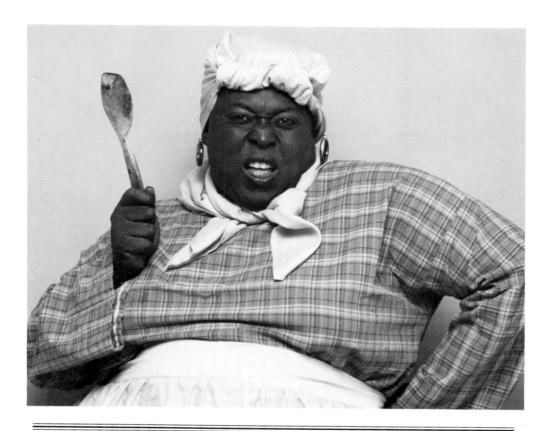

Go ahead, make my day!

"Make sure the chicken is clean . . ."

THEOLA

Child yes! Umum, yeah, yes!

3 large sweet potatoes,
  sliced lengthwise
1 cup cooking oil

1 tbs cinnamon
1 tbs nutmeg

Mix the cinnamon and nutmeg together. Heat the oil. Sprinkle the sweet potatoes with the spices and brown in the oil. Then sit back, take down your hair, slap some Lotty Joseph on the the stereo, and wonder what the poor people be doin'.

"... then brown the chicken West Hollywood style."

GLO

*Honey, this will knock a man away from the table, and once he's down,
throw him your list of demands!*

1 pound fresh black-eyed peas
1 large onion diced
1/2 pound fatback

2 ham hocks
4 large pork neckbones

Throw all the ingredients together in two quarts of boiling water, and cook on medium heat for at least one hour. Even though this dish is very popular with negrae, I wouldn't eat this dish in the Twilight Zone.

LOTTY TAMBINI

This dish is almost as cheap as my husband's wife.

8 ounces medium egg noodles
1/4 cup butter
2 tps sesame seeds

2 tbs poppy seeds
parmesan cheese

Cook the noodles, and mix in the above ingredients. Step back and leave the rest of the cookin' to "Lotty Tambini," 'cause everybody knows those Tambini girls do like to cook.

TINA

Honey, I'm scared of this!

1 pound ground beef
1 medium onion diced
1 can cream of mushroom soup

2 tbs grated celery
1 cup uncooked oats
2 eggs
salt and pepper

This is very simple. Combine all the above ingredients, bake in an oven at 375 degrees for 45 minutes, oh honey, don't be scared.

ARLENE

Oh, but she won't, oh but she does . . .

1 can tuna fish
1 can green peas
1 can condensed cream of
   mushroom soup

1 diced onion
1 can of biscuits (ready to bake)
1 cup diced carrots

You combine all of the ingredients, except the biscuits, in a casserole dish. Put the biscuits on top and bake in an oven on 375 degrees for 15 minutes . . . oh but she has.

Hard times, don't be knockin' at my door.

"It's like the big black hen said to the li'l white rooster,
'Honey you don't be comin' round here like you used ta'."

REVENGE COOKING

REVENGE COOKING, or cooking to get even is a whole new development in cuisinal art. Afterall, poverty will teach you all you need to know about destitution dining and you can go to Miss Crocker to learn how to make something delectable for that boss you're trying to impress. But what about the boss who just told you never to wear corduroys into the office again cause you're creating a fire hazard from the thigh friction? Sara Lee can help you bring your favorite hunk or hunkess to their knees; but what about that one who's drug you through the mill so many times that your panties smell like flour and there's dumplings in your hope chest? When you have to make a meal for a person of this stature, you obviously need a lesson in Revenge Cooking, and for that, my dear, you must come to moi.

I'm experienced in revenge cooking 'cause big mamma has been through some loves that have started out like street gangs, only to sign off like "We the people". For example, Abdul, a no good raghead, camel jockey—told me he loved a heavy hipped woman, had me lying up there in bed eating donuts like they were M&M's, chasing them with whole milk. Come to find out he was dating a heifer on the side that was so skinny she could walk through a harp. When she turned sideways and stuck out her tongue she looked like a zipper. And when this hussy would walk, her bones rattled so much it sounded like three skeletons break dancing on a tin roof. So when I busted up in my boudoir one day and found those two entwined looking like whatever became of the Sinai, I had no choice but to jump in that kitchen and make some *Big Mamma's Blues Birthin' Bisque.*

Or what about the time you have to reward a dear friend for setting you up on a blind date, (with her boss' cousin). She told you he was the strong silent jock type with chiseled features. The last of the red hot trolls. This dogina's face was so pointed he could eat pork-n-beans out of a Pepsi bottle and he played a lot of Pac Man. Silent type? Honey please! Trying to hold a conversation with this man was like trying to do the rhumba with a drunk eel. So you know I had to invite my dear friend over for some *Quiche Dowagiac.*

Or what about the heifer that you just can't stand. You know the one I'm talking about. You would like to rip her head off and spit in her neck, but you can't cause she's a co-worker, or a relative, or a friend of a lover or a lover of a friend. Of course the hussy is running around town, talking out of her behind, smelling up the streets, putting your business in the wind. You know you need a luncheon treat for her.

Of course let us not forget your lesbian friend, from your Medieval

Women's Studies Class, who you asked to watch your apartment while you were away on a long weekend. Needless to say she had some of the girls from heavy equipment school over to watch the playoffs while you were gone and it's been three weeks and you still can't get the smell of beer and pretzels out of the place. Not to mention that one of them had to demonstrate in front of your "Born Again" landlord how she could lick an envelope after it was in the mailbox. What do you do? *Cream of Dyke* is the only answer.

Or what about that hairdresser of yours, you remember. You sent your man to him for a little sprucing up. When he came home he demanded that you perform all of these weird acts of oral copulation, and the minute you refused he ran to your hairdresser for "a trim", came home three hours later and didn't touch you for a week. Not only that, but now the man carries a battery operated blow dryer, redecorates the apartment once a month and is a slave for fashion. Well there's a dish in here that will suit that two timing little hair-burner down on the boulevard.

DISCLAIMER

I want it to be known, right here and now, that I am not taking any responsibility for anything that happens to anyone that uses one of these revenge dishes.

So honey if you lay a little Inez Pendrake on your man and he goes off and re-does your face then it's just a case of C'est pas vrais. Don't come to me for the money for a lift and tuck.

Or if your man should partake of the Negwana Barnes and end up sitting on the toilet until there is nothing left. It's not my fault. You have to realize when you give a man a healthy dose of laxative that when he's done getting it all out there may be nothing left. So don't cry to me. See your astrologer, honey.

So I repeat: use these dishes at your own risk and your own discretion.

NEGWANA BARNES

If the Pilgrims had seen this recipe there would have been another clause in the constitution, honey.

6 ounces bittersweet Baker's chocolate

8 ounces heavy dairy whipping cream

2 packages chocolate laxative

3 ounces brandy

6 ounces shaved Baker's chocolate (semi-sweet)

First you melt the bittersweet chocolate in a double boiler, along with the chocolate laxative, adding the brandy slowly and stirring steadily, until the chocolate has melted.

With an electric mixer beat the whipping cream until it is stiff. This will allow the chocolate to cool down to a luke warmness. This is the trick in making this come out seemingly delectable. You must allow the chocolate to cool to the point where it won't melt the whipped cream but also not be too thick to blend well.

When the whipping cream and the chocolate are ready, fold in the whipping cream. Do not stir, honey, or you might as well have served instant pudding. After you've folded in the whipped cream, gently blend in the shaved baker's chocolate.

This dish tastes absolutely delicious. Your prey will think that it's a chocolate mousse, but we know this mousse is a bear honey.

CALCUTTA, NEW DELHI AND JERSEY

This dish is second in rudeness only to a menage-a-trois between Idi Amin, Princess Anne and Orca.

4 cups mashed potatoes

2 tbs fresh chives

2 tbs bacon bits

1½ cups fresh raw sea urchin

You mix the chives and bacon bits in the mashed potatoes, careful to save some for garnishing the top. Then you mix in the sea urchin, which in color will look just like big hunks of cheddar cheese. After that you garnish the top with the remaining bacon bits and chives.

The dish will appear to be a wonderful au gratin potato dish. But we all know unfortunately, sea urchins taste like creek beds, not cheese.

UTACKI

The last time an American had an oriental experience like this dish was Pearl Harbor.

1 package Nouri seaweed wrap

2 cups cooked rice

1/2 pound carp, filleted for sushi

1 jar wasabi

First of all, cover the carp generously with the wasabi, which is a green oriental mustard that is hotter than a ten buck Cadillac. Spread some wasabi on the strips of nouri. Then cover it with rice. At one edge, atop the rice, place some strips of carp and then roll it up like you were rolling a joint. Cut the roll into bite sized chop stick pieces and slap it on the table with some soy sauce and ginger and sit back and prepare for the sweetness that is revenge.

"When a man doesn't keep up with his homework.
A woman has got to get the answers the best way she can.
And believe me . . . there are better ways!"

CREAM OF DYKE

Though this doesn't sound that bad, nothing is more offensive to a lesbian than something warm, white, salty and slippery sliding down her throat.

1 pound tofu

1 quart cream
2 tsp salt

It's also a very simple recipe. All you have to do is to combine the above ingredients and heat in a large saucepan until they are warm, not hot mind you, just warm.

QUICHE DOWAGIAC

This is for that dream quarterback in your life who faded back with the football of your love and fumbled . . ., honey.

1 ready to bake single pie crust
1/2 cup pork brains
1/2 pound diced okra

6 eggs
1 dash salt
1 dash pepper

First of all you beat the eggs well. Then you pour them in the pie crust. You mix the brains with the okra and add them to the pie. Put in the dash of salt and pepper.

Bake this lovely little number on 350 for 20 minutes or until the eggs have hardened and serve it with a sly smile.

RUDACIOUS TATA

Honey this drink is grittier than the southwest corner of a sheep's behind.

2 packages cocoa mix
2 trays ice cubes

1/2 fifth of Sambucca
2 tsp cinnamon

Combine the above ingredients together in a blender and blend until the ice is broken up into a palatable size. You'll just love it. I mean you'll just love the look on his face when he takes his first drink. It's perfect for the man suffering from a case of bottle fatigue.

BEETS JUANITA

This is a dish for the man who just did his homesteading somewhere else after spending years cultivating your Paw Paw patch.

1 can sliced beets
2 bottles tabasco sauce

8 ounces sliced jicama
6 tbs ground cayenne pepper

Sprinkle the jicama over the beets in baking dish. Pour the tabasco sauce over the vegetables then sprinkle liberally with the cayenne. After that bake in the oven on 475 for a half an hour or until the tabasco sauce is absorbed into the beets like a tangy marinade. "Vengence, sayeth the Lord."

YULIIS'S SPROUT MOUSSE

This is for the man who showed up so late for your date that he passed himself going home.

1 pound sprouts
1/4 pound of blended comfrey root

2 packages of plain gelatin

Make the gelatin according to the recipe then fold in the comfrey root and the sprouts. You can find comfrey root at your health food store, and like Yuliis, this dish is extremely light and very airy.

PRUNELLA AGNES BETH

This is for the man who's slammed the door in the face of decency!

1 pound stewed prunes
4 cups cooked rice
1 cup shredded cooked beets
1 dash cinnamon

1 dash garlic
6 fertilized eggs
1 tbs salt
1 tbs double action baking powder

Okay honey, you take the above ingredients and combine them in a big bowl, mix them well. Then you put them in a baking dish and bake on a high temperature for about 30 minutes.

Honey, this will open the door back up. Even if it has to go via wall.

VOILA BEOUF!

C'est pas vrais! Mais non! The french would say to this dish.

1 pound cubed beef
2 cups sugar
1 cup molasses

3 boxes cloves
2 quarts water

Bring the water to a boil. Then think about what the sucker, suckess, or suckee has done to you and throw that beef up in the water and add the remaining ingredients. Before I'd eat this dish I'd rather be next in line for the throne of Uganda.

FLOSSIE SUE PAUL COBBLER

This is for the man who played you like a second-hand cello.

1 pound diced mountain oysters
2 cups grits
1 large deep dish pastry crust

1 can mandarin orange slices
2 tsp basil

First you cook the grits according to the instructions on the box.

Then you line a pastry dish with the pastry crust. Put the diced mountain oysters (see glossary for the low "T" on these girls) at the bottom. Then you cover with the orange slices; pour the grits on top, after stirring in the basil. Bake this for 45 minutes and there you have it. Pestilence, in the form of a pie.

WIG WEARIN' CONNIE BISQUE

She stole your man, never returned your dress, and is trying to give 'em your hair style at the club. . . . she screams for this dish.

1 quart water
8 ounces fresh mackerel,
  blended in the food processor

1 can peaches,
  blended in the food processor
1 tbs sage

Combine the above ingredients in a large pot. Bring that pot to a boil. Put on your black dress, 'cause you are doing devilment.

Cook this for a long, long time. . . . and then slap her on the table and watch the despised get even uglier.

NO NECK NANCY ALFREDO

Mamma Mia! Whata rude Tia.

1 pound pork liver
1 package spaghetti

1 can tomato paste
1 jar olives

Boil the spaghetti noodles and pork livers in a quart of water.

After you do that, drain the water. Mix in the pork livers which you should chop into little pieces and the olives.

This is some terrible "T", honey.

HI HO

This dish is so greasy you'll have to tie it to your teeth to chew it.

8 avocado halves
6 ounces cornmeal
2 tbs flour

2 cups water
2 cups hog lard (any shortening
  will do if you can't find hog lard,
  but hog lard is the best for
  this dish)

This dish is deep fried avocados smothered in gravy. Can you imagine! First you rinse the avacados then you bread them with the corn meal by rolling them in it.

Meanwhile you should be heating up the hog lard in a skillet. After the hog lard is hot, slap those avocados in there and fry them. After they're golden brown, take them out. Pour away all but two tablespoons of the lard. Put in the flour, brown it, add the water, simmer until it's gravy and then put the avocados in the gravy and cook on a low heat for five minutes and serve.

MUGU GAI GRACIOUS

The last time Germany and Japan teamed up for something like this it took the H Bomb to straighten it out.

2 cups chopped bratwurst
1 cup bamboo shoots
1 cup water chestnuts

2 tbs Mongolian hot oil
1/2 cup sauerkraut
1/2 cup sweet and sour sauce

Combine the first five ingredients together in a wok and cook until you're tired of dealing with it.

Then you throw the sweet and sour sauce on and let it get warm and serve it.

It will be visions of Rommel and Togo let me tell you.

CHOLA

When attitude is just not enough.....go for this one, the name speaks for itself. This dish will definitely get your guest to say, "okay let's step out in the alley maricone....and what will it be...knives or glass."

1 pint vanilla ice cream
1 box cayenne pepper
1/4 bottle food coloring (red)

1 handful jalapeno peppers
1 cup skim milk

This, like most cholas, is very simple. You just blend the above ingredients together until they are smooth.

Then you invite your victim over for some type of strenuous exercise. When they're all hot, sweaty and thirsty lay this Yucatan delight on them.

INEZ PENDRAKE

This recipe is tackier than wearing sweat socks with high heels, which is something an Inez would do.

Peanut butter
jelly (mint)

Bread (rye)
Plain wrap tuna fish

This is for you girls who have found out that while you were at home homemaking your man was out creepin' with Sally and Sue, Esther and Robert too.

This is for his lunch. It's very simple. Spread the peanut butter on one slice of bread, the jelly on the other. Put the tuna fish in the middle. Smush the bread together so the flavors meld, so to speak, and put it in his lunch pail with that cigarette butt covered with lipstick that's not even close to your shade. He'll know not to come home without roses, excuses, promises and plans.

Sinskey

Gonna hit that low road in these high heel shoes
Totin' a suitcase, full of blues.

OYSTERS AMIN

Imagine Idi Amin and an oyster in the same room. That in itself is revenge.

8 oysters on the half shell   1 cup prepared tapioca pudding

Cover each oyster with tapioca pudding and you're done. This is when you're mad but you hate to waste the time to get even, but you know you must.

"Those lips . . . those eyes . . . those hips . . . those thighs."

NAOMI NASH

Like a true Naomi, this dish is too, too rude.

1 roasting chicken
1 box curry
1 can chocolate sauce

1/2 pound diced beef liver
1 cup cauliflower
1 cup kidney beans

Rub the chicken with the curry and then cover with the chocolate sauce. Stuff the remaining ingredients inside the chicken and bake on 375 for 45 minutes.

Serve this to your mother in law. Tell her it was a recipe you got out of the magazine that she gave you a subscription to last year... "Better Homes and Waifs."

BERNARDOLAISE (HOY VEY)

Honey this is for the friend who set you up on a blind date with a man who hasn't been in the arms of a woman since his baptism.

1/2 pound ground chicken liver, cooked
1/2 pound ground calves liver, cooked
1/2 pound ground beef liver, cooked

2 large onions (fried, and blotted, then ground)
6 hard boiled eggs, ground
1½ bottles of castor oil

As if you were making the Beverly Hills Mousse, combine the above ingredients together. Mix the Castor Oil in well, as it has no taste, and will take on the taste of the chopped liver. All will seem well until late that night, when your phone rings and your victim says, "Hoy Vey!....." As you might have guessed this dish is a *cheap* trick.

HOT LICKS BOMBAY

Before I'd eat this dish I'd allow a man to drag me by my beautiful hair down to a construction site in Mobile, Alabama, tie me to a Porta-John and make me fall in love with a steel driving hammer.

1 pound of diced tongue
   (Beef, lamb or pork)
6 ounces cayenne pepper

1/2 pound curry
2 cups marischino cherries
4 cups water

First you boil the tongue in the water, with the curry and the cayenne until all of the water evaporates.

Then you take the remaining tongue and spices out of the pot, careful to scrape the sides so you get as much flavor as possible. Put in a dish and cover with the cherries and bake for 10 minutes. You might just add a little water to make a gravy sauce on this dastardly act of cuisinal madness.

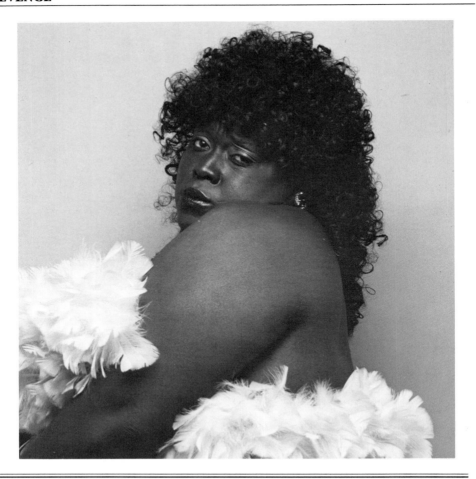

Nothing wrong, but something ain't quite right.

BIG MAMMA'S BLUES BIRTHIN' BISQUE

If you think this is hot on the way in, wait until she comes out, and honey she will be coming out.

2 quarts quinine water   1 pound jalapeno peppers
1 pound prunes   4 tbs cayenne pepper (ground)

Put the above ingredients into a large pot and stew on a slow low heat until the ingredients cook apart and the mixture has the consistency of a good tomato soup. 'Cause when she comes out, honey, that's what she's gonna look like.

ROXIE

This will make a victim's ears fold back like a Pit Bull in a wind tunnel.

1 package linguini cooked   1 cup candied yams
1/2 cup mustard   1 jar hot dog relish

Mix the above ingredients together and serve as if nothing is wrong. Honey!!!!

PANDORA MAE

This will make a man tear his face up like a cat trying to cover up nuclear waste on a tin roof.

1 carton plain yogurt
2 cups buttermilk
4 tbs linseed oil
1/2 cup olive oil
1 cup any wine with a screw cap
2 figs

1 cup comfrey root
1/2 cup salt
1 avocado peel
1 cup lentils
1/2 pound Bok choy

In an industrial strength blender blend the above ingredients and serve after they've reached a smooth consistency.

Serve it to a health food junky and tell them it's super good for them and watch them suffer through it.

BERG, STEIN AND WHOLESALE

This dish could make Jews outlaw money.

8 ounces cream cheese
4 ounces ham fat
2 tbs mayonnaise
1/2 cup cheese whip

1 cup juiced squid
1 bottle clam juice
4 bagels

Take the bagels and soak them in clam juice. Allow them to dry overnight. Then blend the remaining ingredients together and spread them on the halved bagels, which you halved when you soaked them in clam juice.

Serve them as just your everyday nosh.

LUCINDA LOUISE

This dish is so rude if you put a door on it, it would be a trailer.

1 package strawberry gelatin
1/4 cup diced raw white potatoes

1/4 cup diced rhubarb

It's simple, yet more to the point than most marriages. All you have to do is follow the instructions for making gelatin and as the gelatin begins to congeal fold in the potatoes and rhubarb.

Imagine this: He's suffered through a revenge entree, and here comes the gelatin. Now who could ruin gelatin? He sighs a sigh of relief. It's over. He takes a bite and honey, it's only just begun.

MISS TIJUANA, 1962

*Honey this dish is at least twice as rude as the woman who held
that dubious title.*

1 large soft flour tortilla
1 can yams
1 package okra

1 can sardines
1 pound anchovies

Mix the last four ingredients together and put into the tortilla.

Fold the tortilla like a burrito and honey. . . . burrrrrritttto!

It's perfect!!

EGGS BELINDA

The only way this egg dish could get any ruder would be if you got Princess Anne to lay the eggs.

1 cup diced ground hog mawls
2 poached eggs (twelve minutes)

2 english muffin halves
1 patty margarine

The hog mawl should be cooked. Boiling them is fine. Melt the margarine over the english muffins, pour on the hog mawls generously and then top with that 12 minute egg. That oughta do it.

And if you're really mad, garnish with a radish.

CREAM OF CLEVELAND-SAIGON STYLE

Anything with Cleveland in the name must be terrible....it's the law child.

1/4 pound dates
1/2 pound figs
2 cups diced watermelon
3 bananas

2 bay leaves
1/4 pound brazil nuts
Crispy deep fried oriental noodles
1 quart buttermilk

Mix the first six ingredients in the buttermilk and then pour them over the crispy noodles.

Honey this "T" is lower than whale graves. It's almost as low as Stephen and those sleazy San Francisco floozies at that I-Beam.

CHRISTIE COME LATELY

This dish will make you slap Bambi.

1 lamb breast
1 bottle clam juice
1 jar tomato paste

1 cup flour
2 cups hog lard or cooking oil
2 cups clam sauce

First you heat the grease on the stove in a large frying pan. Then you cut the lamb breast into pieces and flour it.

You put it into the oil and fry it honey. Then after it is fried, you take it out. You mix the clam juice with the tomato paste and pour it over the lamb.

Then you heat up the clam sauce, and pour it over the lamb. Serve it with a side of grease.

WEST HOLLYWOOD LOAF

This is for all you girls who have lost your man in the Hollywood Hills, or as we call them "Swish Alps."

12 ounces anchovie paste
16 ounces generic beer
8 ounces cooked linguini noodles
16 ounces mackerel

2 cups rice puffs
8 ounces tomato paste
1 tbs salt
2 cups yellow corn meal

Combine the above ingredients and shape it into a loaf. Put this in the oven and cook at 400⁰ until she has the texture of a seedy dinge-queen.

Now, if you want some real, genuine West Hollywood flavor, you must follow the all too trendy West Hollywood technique. First you make this dish wearing no less than five different designer labels. You must also wear at least one pair of sunglasses, preferably two (one for your eyes and one for your coiff . . . which has been blown dry, of course). And for that true West Hollywood style, when you slap this trash on the table throw your head back and believe you're *real* pretty.

DIVINE

If you really want to get revenge on someone, what could be worse than something old, white, wrinkled and stringy, called Divine.

1 pound tripe
16 ounces dry, old tofu

12 ounces mayonnaise
2 tbs tartar

First you combine the last 3 ingredients. Stir them well, then you pour that mixture over the tripe and bake for 2 hours at 350⁰. This dish is *almost* as rude as its name.

PALMER PARK

Honey, this dish could make Queen Elizabeth break-dance with B.B. King.

1 can biscuits
1 cup black-eyed peas
1 cup diced squid
1 cup dried pork liver

1 can French onion soup
1 cup spinach (cooked)
1 lb. salmon eggs

Mix all the ingredients together except the biscuits. Now pour the mixture in a casserol dish, put the biscuits on top and bake in the oven at 375⁰ until the biscuits are brown, and this religious experience will have your victim praying to the porcelin god in no time.

APPENDIX

·

SHOPPING TIPS

·

THE FINAL "T"

·

GLOSSARY

·

INDEX OF RECIPES

·

ACKNOWLEDGEMENTS

·

Sinskey

That supermarket will wear on a girl.

SHOPPING TIPS

THE FIRST THING to remember is never go shopping when you're hungry. Honey, I did that one time and came home with a fifty-pound bag of bamboo shoots, a case of water chestnuts and a gallon of soy sauce. To this very day I can't watch Kung Fu movies.

As long as we're on the subject of spending foolishly, we might as well discuss spending wisely. If it's possible, you should plan menus for the entire week before you go to the store. Make a shopping list and stick to it, honey.

You should also remember if you buy foods that are in season they're gonna be a lot cheaper. It's just like blondes in Hollywood—they're a lot cheaper here than, in Tel-Aviv, because the market is flooded with them, whereas in Tel-Aviv, they're a delicacy. Sorta like quail eggs.

Always remember to check the dates on products so that you're sure you're getting the freshest food available. Unless, of course, you're budget-shopping. In which case you should always look for the products that have been light-damaged and marked down because they've turned darker. The fact of the matter is that meats in America today have so many artificial additives a little browning from the lights is hardly gonna hurt you. To snub your nose at red meat discounted because it's turned brown is like telling a one-night stand your last name in the morning—at that point, what does it matter?

The second thing to remember when you are going grocery shopping is that stores are open to the public, and that means anybody can go there. So beware. Honey let me tell you about the time I ran into drunken Yolanda Bryant in the pastry aisle, staggering like she was balancing her hope chest on her nose. Her eyes were so red the communist party had pasted a membership card on her forehead.

Child she had been on a three week drinking binge, and when she began to sober up she realized that she had married a 95 year old man. Honey that old man busted up in the store behind Yolanda (lookin' like the Ho Chi Minh Trail) talking about his new bride and Yolanda fainted and fell up into the Bundt cakes, spun around over into the self rising flour, slid down into the corn meal and fell on my purse!

Girl, that old man was on Yolanda like an unmarried Jewess on a single lawyer. It was worse than Sandy Duncan on a wheat thin. That old man went to fanning Yolanda and carrying on and his old bones got to rattling so much it sounded like two tin men doing the jitterbug in a Wok. And every time Yolanda would come to, she'd take one look at that old man and she'd fall out again...right back on my purse! And I had three fifths of Mad dog in my purse for my nerves. Honnneyyy! She broke 'em both. And when those bottles broke. . .Yolanda smelled that Mad dog and came hither like a young soldier coming home from the war. Turned my purse up to her mouth like it was a beer can. Drank all of that Mad dog and spit out the pieces of broken glass, my eyebrow pencil and my powder puff like they were seeds from a grape. That woman is not well.

I stepped back and slapped my hands upon my luscious hips and looked at Yolanda, laying down there next to the grits, drunk as a menopausal coota, off of *my* Mad dog, I mean nerve medicine. I thanked God, for her, that I was a church-going woman.

Then I thought again about how hard I had come by that nerve medicine and I was forced to lay down my religion and pick up a stick of frozen chocolate chip cookie dough out of the freezer section. Honey I beat that ugly heifer like she was a rented rug. Child I wopped her until a hymn came to her. Girl I started at her ears, and went due south, then out west and back up north via the east. I beat that woman's drawers off, down her legs, up her back, over the top of her head, across her face, into her mouth, down her throat, out her buttois, up her legs and back on her behind.

And do you know that heifer liked it.

Another important thing to remember: don't be afraid to ask the butcher to do his job. It's his job to cut things and shave things. Butchers get into it. It's a fetish. And if they get ugly with you? If they get ugly with you, tell them you'll jump behind that meat counter and make them fall in love with a summer sausage. That always works for me.

"A girl does not stand in line in lamé."

THE FINAL "T"

BEFORE I go any further, let me explain the meaning of the word "T." T has a rich heritage. It comes from the slave women. You see, when the slave women were serving the old belles of the antebellum south, they used to eavesdrop on the gossip at the tea parties. The belles would, of course, be gossiping about what Rebecca was doing with Beauregard, and what Ellie Ann had been rumored to have done with those frisky ol' Merrill boys.

Well, sometimes the slave women would become so engrossed in the gossip that they would stop paying attention to what they were doing and spill the tea. And when they got back to the kitchen, the cooks and helpers would ask the servers, "Well, did you spill the tea, girl?" Meaning, of course, was the gossip good? Hence the expression, "spill the T."

Then came the war, and a ravaged and ragged south turned its weak and battered eyes towards a dark and dismal sky, and a silence fell upon Atlanta, a silence more frightening than the thunder of the Yankee cannons. . .ooops wrong story. . .What happened was the freeing of the slaves, and a lot of the slave women went into "domestic work" where they continued to use the expression "spill the tea" to mean "give me the juice" or the jist of it. Well, most of the rich white women's sons grew up to be gay. And the rich queens brought the expression to the gay bars. At the bars it was shortened to "T," meaning, "pertinent facts," "jist of," "skinny on," "story," etc. Now there's even low T and high T. High T being good news or good information, and Low T bad news, or terrible facts.

For example, Queen Elizabeth is some Low T. But the fact that she's the Queen of England and not the United States is some High T. See what I mean?

So here's the final T. In this lil' ol' book you have some of my simple, yet delectable recipes. They're easy. Even my girlfriend, Maxine can make them. And God knows that Maxine is a lush. Honey, Maxine tried to donate some blood to the Red Cross and they found an olive in her blood!

Even some of my "older" girlfriends, like Miss Burr, can make these. . . and, honey, Miss Burr's insurance policy covers Indian raids. So you know that her eyesight and energy is not that great anymore. I mean there aren't that many people who can say that they knew Baskin Robbins when it didn't have but two flavors. Nevertheless, Miss Burr has no problems with these recipes.

It's only fair, and moral, that I warn you again that these dishes are not to be taken lightly. Not to be played with. These dishes are for serious business. I used one of the motive dishes to soften the heart of Amanda

Hall (my old boss at Miss Nancy's Knit and Sew) and, honey, I'm telling you, Amanda Hall could swallow a glass of water and spit out a handful of crushed ice cubes.

So there you have it girls! Here they are, the dishes that a girl needs to do what a girl has got to do. Let's face it, in this day and age a good man is hard to come by. It's some sad but true T, the good men are either gay, married, unemployed or only interested in getting in your "paw paw patch." A girl has got to have a little defense. Good cookin' is it. It's as proven as the fact that fat girls have to be nice. Mais No! Remember be careful with these dishes cause, honey, they'll make a man run off in two different directions screaming your praises.

Honey, let me give you the real tea.

"Ain't this some uncomprehensible demoralization?"

GLOSSARY

WHY have I written a glossary for this cookbook? Well honey there are several reasons, the main one being I'm from Detroit, (extreme suburban Detroit, Dowagiac,) and I just ain't got the time. You see it be like this: My friend's father died and for his inheritance he got a quarter of a million dollars...my father died, and I got my mother. So that leaves me with my mother, my dog and a 60 inch waist, so honey my hands are full and I don't have the time to have you ringing my phone off the hook asking me what I mean by this and what's that supposed to mean. Understand?

I suppose that's a terrible attitude from an artistic point of view. And yes many times, Randy West, detail Nazi that he is, has thrown his hands in the air, looked helplessly to his staff, who sat quietly, shivering under a dark cloak of chagrin, as Randy screamed, "Art! Doesn't this large black woman from the southland understand? Doesn't she know art?"

At last, dear Randy, I'm going to answer that question. Yes, sugar puddin, big mamma knows Art...Art from Forrest Lawn and as a matter of fact he called up here this morning and if I don't make another payment on my late daddy's grave...Art says...up he comes. So honey, I got to get on up the street and get this book on the shelves. Do you know what I mean?

Of course you know what I mean... therefore you know why I've included this glossary. Not to mention that while I've been away working on this masterpiece in cuisinal guidance, a little beach bunny from one of the lower rent Orange county beaches has managed to sneak up to LA and snatch Macho Puff away from me...bless his little Italian soul. Did I say little...mia culpa...dah'ling. Anyway big mamma's got some retrieving to do...so I had to write this glossary for you.

Not to mention that the love warriors are sitting down in Laguna Beach with nothing but their war clubs and memories of how sweet the smell of my perfume use to be. So you know I've got to leave this typewriter be for a while and go on a mission of mercy honey...and I mean mercy, mercy, mercy! I'm serious you just don't know those love warriors. It's a den of TWP! There's enough virile manhood up in that house to go to war with. I guess that's why they're called the love warriors huh? Well big mamma has gotta get on down there and bring some peace to those boys...and you know I'm a woman of piece.

And another thing. Cooking is an art honey, like sculpting or playing bid whisk. It's not so much what you put together or how long you let it marinade. No child. It's all in the attitude. There's a difference between laying something in a pan and slapping something in a pan. When you slap something in a pan it effects the flavor gnodes of the food and consequently the food tastes better. Do you know what a big woman means?

Not only that being a good cook is not just a characteristic, it's an aura, a being, a way of life, a vocation, a calling, a destiny. So you can't just learn a few good recipes and call it a day. That would be like a monk learning a couple of prayers and then getting on up the street. You have to live the life. In order to cook these delectable dishes you have to talk to the food in a language that food understands. You have to talk like me; pop your dress tail, like a big woman thang pops her dress tail. you have to cross your big luscious legs honey and talk trash child. And that's what this glossary will teach you is how to talk trash . . . like moi.

Art	1. Something Randy says I don't have.
Buttois	1. Rear End. 2. Ancient Russian temple guard.
C'est ne pas vrais	1. (Literally) It is not true. 2. (idiomatically) Lies and vicious rumours...honey this "T" is lower than the price of ham in Jerusalem.
Chitlins	1. Southern most intestinal tract of a pig.
Collard Greens	1. Leafy green vegetable that is cooked with ham hocks and neckbones and kale. 2. Reason black women are good at doing the dirty deed.
Contraband	1. Something the government won't allow you to have. 2. Something you can't live without.
Fatback	1. Fat meat cured in salt used in soul and southern cooking.
Gaffers	1. Macho men who do the lighting on sets and know where to find narcotics at all times. 2. Reason why dejected women should go on living.
Goat Mawls	1. The stomach of a goat, most often used in Himalayan mountain cuisine. 2. Ugly women who hang around gangsters.
Good Gocious	1. Hammercy. 2. This dish is finishing cooking.
Grits	1. Farina looking little things, made from grinding hominy. 2. People who live in trailors.
Grips	1. Big strong men that move cameras on sets that usually don't have much in the hayloft but have full silos for days. 2. Another reason why dejected women have to go on.
Heifer	1. A tawdry vixen. 2. A dish of substance. 3. Moi.
Hog Mawls	1. Stomach of pigs. 2. Fat women who hang around gangsters.
Hold Office	1. Leave the kitchen immediately. 2. Read some beads.
Honkess	1. A person who has extremely straight hair and an inability to do the dirty deed. 2. Someone who would be weighing up peanuts at the dimestore for the rest of their life if not for plumbers, carpenters and truck drivers. 3. Device in the bill of a goose used for speaking.
Honkette	1. The offspring of a honkess and a blue collar worker. 2. A short curt reply from a goose.
Honkine	1. Someone whose face looks like a human brain: an old caucasian. 2. A small device in the throat of a goose used for sending honk waves to the honkess.
Italian Stallion	1. A final reason for dejected women to go on.
Jewess	1. Homely beast with large nostrils designed for sniffing out wholesale outlets, stray coins, gaudy dresses and day old bagel stands. 2. sad "T".

JAP	1. Reason God invented credit cards, plastic surgeons, and Mexican housekeepers. 2. A predatory growth that appears on the arms and wallets of lawyers, doctors and accountants.
Jewette	1. A child capable of buying bubble gum wholesale from gum ball machines.
Jewine	1. One of the original inventors of wholesale.
Kale	1. A curly green leafy vegetable. 2. Prestigious negro college.
Kool-aid	1. A cocktail mixer (good for scotch drinks when Revenge cooking). 2. A walk-man.
Mad dog	1. Cooking wine. 2. Unmarried white woman over 50 years of age.
Man	1. One eyed, purple veined, moisture and heat seeking wand of destruction that is accompanied by two arms and two legs. 2. The reason dejected girls should not go on.
Mountain oyster	1. The gonads of a bull. 2. Strong argument for vegetarianism.
Mousette	1. A bite size mousse. 2. An Austrian street walker.
Muscatel	1. A Negro blood type. 2. Fine dinner wine.
Nebraska	1. Home of Kathy M. 2. A land where men are men and women are grateful (the reason Kathy lives there). 3. A large cornfield between New York and LA.
Neckbones	1. Neck portion of a pig used in good cooking . 2. Attributes desperate skinny white women refer to as beauty traits.
Negress	1. The reason God invented welfare. 2. Very fertile creature, with little hair and lots of derriere. 3. A place where basketball players come from.
Negrettes	1. Juvenile delinquents.
Negrines	1. People who call themselves colored. 2. The reason God invented watermelon.
Pecs	1. The part of the man you squeeze after the ego and before the wallet. 2. Hummingbird gonads.
Peruvian Marching Powder	1. The reason the people in South America don't look like the people in Ethiopia. 2.Magical powder that will get beautiful girls to go out with overweight balding guys.
Pinch	1. A small measure used in cooking. 2. A Polish midget who manages prostitutes.
Polk salad	1. Spinach-like vegetable that grows in the woods. 2. State bird of Mississippi.
Shallot	1. Onion type vegetable. 2. Fallopian tube of a Yak.

"You know there must be a word for this."

Slap

1. A cooking technique; the way one moves food from one place to another.

Stretch pants

1. The reason God made trailer parks, casseroles, country music and beehive hairdos. 2. Indiana women's reason to go on living.

T

1. The "T" on "T" is in the final "T". 2. A letter in the English alphabet.

Tad

1. A cooking measure: tiny amount 2. Cute boy on "All My Children" who doesn't deserve Hilary after what he did to Liza, Marion Colby, Dotty and Edna.

Tripe

1. Cow stomach. 2. Eskimo concubine.

Voila Beouf

1. (Literally) Here's the beef. 2. (Idiomatic) Nothing likes a bone but a dog and he don't want it when he can get some meat.

Waspess

1. A honkess with a trust fund. 2. Female reproductive organ of the North American wasp.

Waspette

1. A child who owns stock in companies that he doesn't know exists. 2. The reason God invented private schools.

Waspine

1. Living proof that there ain't no justice. 2. A person whose name is on the side of a tall building, and a swarthy person's paycheck. 3. A tubular organ inside of a moth that is used to make imitation wasp sounds to ward off moth killing bees.

REVENGE

DESTITUTION

MOTIVE

*Read this sister, heed and weep
and if you can't read, weep anyway*

SEDUCTION

ACKNOWLEDGEMENTS

THEY say behind every great man there is a woman. Well behind every great woman-thang there are a few great men (figuratively speaking). I would like to dedicate this book to the great men who were behind me or basically all the business men, sailors, truckers, lawyers and doctors that I used to know before I became an authoress/actress/mannequin extraordinaire.

Finally in a serious vein. . .in the preceding pages I have made fun of Jews, Blacks, Whites, old people, children, Orientals, Chicanos, men, women, gays, straights, skinnies, fatties, blondes, brunettes, redheads, handicapped people, baldies, foreigners, Republicans and paupers.

But only as a part of an effort to give you all laughter, because it is by laughing at ourselves and each other that we are able to muster the courage to grow, and it is in that growth that we will come together as one people, spared from the poverty of factions and blessed with the wealth of indivisability; it is in that unity that we will find the strength that is necessary for us to survive.

I would like to thank the people whose unwaivering support has made it possible for me to bring this gift of laughter to you. A special thanks to:

Daniel J. Pyne, Randy West, Bill Conway, David Lindsey, Rune Kaptur, Barbara Hadra and Daddy.

I would also like to make a special offering of these pages to the people who taught me that pain and the need for laughter don't know Beverly Hills from Harlem and that there are no victims, only volunteers. Especially for:

Cynthia Burr, Jane Ackley, Debbie Dalton, Lynn Havel, Stephen Potter, Gerrie Heskett, Elaine Vaughan, Barbara Hokanson-Hicks, Greg Clary, Roger Lachowicz, Shawn Pechette, Valerie Holt, Yuliis Ruval, Deirdre Naughton and Mamma.

*"No great meal be finished
'till the cleaning be done."*